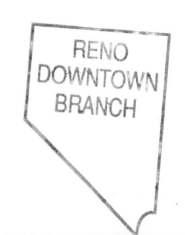

true blue

true blue

the real stories behind NYPD BLUE

David Milch and Det. Bill Clark

william morrow and company, inc.
new york

It is the policy of William Morrow and Company, Inc., and its imprints and affiliates, recognizing the importance of preserving what has been written, to print the books we publish on acid-free paper, and we exert our best efforts to that end.

Library of Congress Cataloging-in-Publication Data

Milch, David, 1945–
    True blue : the real stories behind *NYPD Blue* / David Milch and
  Bill Clark.
      p.   cm.
    ISBN 0–688–14081–5
    1. New York (N.Y.).   Police Dept.—Case studies.   I. Clark, Bill,
  1944– . II. Title.
  HV8148.N5M53   1995
  363.2'09747'1—dc20   95–18919
                                                            CIP

Printed in the United States of America

First Edition

1 2 3 4 5 6 7 8 9 10

BOOK DESIGN BY CAROLINE CUNNINGHAM

To the memory of my brother John

—B.C.

To Rita, my wife, and our beloved children, Elizabeth, Ben, and Olivia

—D.M.

true blue

Kathleen Farley on the steps of her
neighbor's home as police arrive
*Photo originally appeared in the New
York* Daily News

chapter 1

The morning she died, Kathleen Farley had a backache that kept her home from work. The backache got her murdered, because a skel junkie broke in to rob her house and when she heard the noise and came downstairs the junkie strangled and killed her.

This was Bill, talking to me at P. J. Clarke's restaurant, a steak joint in midtown Manhattan where in years past when he was off-duty as a detective he had worked as a bouncer. Bill and I ate in more steak joints the months we were getting to know each other than I've eaten in all the rest of my life.

Steven Bochco and the network executives at ABC were at an impasse over what kind of street language and how much nudity would be allowed on the new series about New York City cops that Steven and I had created, the first two hours of which I'd just written. My personality makes me a liability in those kinds of discussions, so while Steven and the network negotiated, I flew from Los Angeles to New York to research more episodes. A friend, Michael Daly, a newspaper columnist who'd written about New York City cops for twenty years, had given me Bill's name, saying Bill was the best detective he knew. We'd met an hour before in Bill's office in the homicide squad of the 112th Precinct in Queens and driven together to the restaurant in Manhattan. I'd asked him to tell me about a good case, and Bill started talking about Kathleen Farley.

This woman's last conversation was with her husband, who had just gotten to his job and called home to see how she was feeling, and she told him her back was a little better and she was going to make meatballs for dinner and she'd freeze some more for them to have another day. It must've been right after she hung up from this call that she heard a noise and went downstairs and saw the guy who'd broken in through the basement window.

The skel laid hands on her, strangled her till she lost consciousness, then he went upstairs and started to ransack the dressers looking for money and jewelry and whatever else he could carry away with him and sell for dope. And then he heard the woman stirring downstairs, in his confession he said he heard Kathleen Farley starting to come up the stairs, so he went back down and laid hands on her again till she passed out, then he found her purse and cut the strap off to wrap around her neck, but the strap was too short, so he cut an electrical cord and used that, he got her facedown with his knee in her back to get leverage and he strangled her with the cord, then he went back upstairs and finished rummaging and stealing.

Now this prick comes back down and stops and takes a knife from the kitchen and slits the woman's throat as he goes by her on his way out of the house. What he does, the woman was just about out of her misery, but by him slitting her throat, a little air began to get into her lungs through the wound below the electrical cord, so when the skel left she was getting enough air where she could drag herself up and outside her house to try to get help.

Kathleen Farley went to her neighbor's door that she knew for fourteen years and rang the doorbell, but when her neighbor came to the door the neighbor didn't recognize her because her face had gone blue-black from the air being cut off and there was blood pouring out her neck and she was holding the kitchen knife the skel had used to cut her throat, and the neighbor was frightened and closed the door on her. This was a woman who was close friends with Kathleen Farley and felt terrible afterward—she came to the courtroom every day when this guy was on trial and told me she'd never forgive herself for not recognizing Kathleen Farley while she went staggering out into the street trying to stop a car to get someone to help her.

People kept running to phones to call 911—there's five or six calls came in within a minute or so of each other—and *meanwhile one of the cars she nearly bumped into and where the guy had pulled over to call it in, this guy turned out to be a New York Daily News photographer, and he snapped pictures of this woman in the street and as the patrol cars came to assist her, and those pictures wound up in the paper and wound up jamming the skel up who did this to her, because I found the paper opened to the picture in the skel's shitbox of a filthy apartment after the guy had run off and that's when I knew I was looking for the right guy.*

Bill considered me as he talked. He'd agreed to our meeting because of his relationship with Michael, who'd sat up with Bill through the long night after Bill's younger brother had died (we'd tell the story of Bill's younger brother in an episode about Detective James Martinez in the middle of our first season). Also, he knew that Steven and I had worked on the police series *Hill Street Blues*, parts of which he had admired. Still, Bill understood that the realities of TV storytelling and his own job were different, and I could feel him weighing what it was prudent or useful to say.

On my side of the table, I knew I'd just gotten lucky. The two episodes of *NYPD Blue* I'd already written had established the characters and complicated relationship of Detectives John Kelly and Andy Sipowicz and other personalities in the world of the 15th Detective Squad. But I'd painted them in broad strokes; I needed a better sense of the world's specific rhythms and textures. And here was Bill, with his hard-minded details and almost defiant pride in his job.

When we got to Kathleen Farley's house the uniform cops had already taken her to Flushing Hospital. I got her husband's phone number from the neighbor woman who had turned her away, and I called her husband and identified myself and said there was a problem at home, his wife had been hurt and he should come to the house and I would take him to the hospital.

In married-woman homicides, your first look is at the husband. With husbands, though, it's usually a sudden passionate act, so in this case the woman's being strangled with a cord lowered my suspicion. Then, how the husband responded when he got our call and came back to the house, his reaction when he went through the ransacked dresser upstairs to see what was missing and telling me about his talk with his wife on the telephone, that all seemed credible to me. A problem a lot of detectives have is they don't want to believe they've got a case to solve so they go to the closest person at hand.

Kathleen Farley's sister had arrived by this time, and when I took her and the husband to the hospital the doctors told Joseph Farley his wife had lost so much blood before they'd gotten to transfuse her that her organs were all damaged, they had her on life support but he should prepare for the worst.

We left the husband and sister at the hospital and went back to Utopia Parkway to extend our canvass, talking to various neighbors, and when Mr. Farley stopped back briefly from the hospital we inventoried with him what was missing from the house—it was a school ring, a diamond engagement ring, and some bracelets. We also did background checks at the husband's place of work and his wife's. The other workers all said they had a happy marriage and were good people.

Our break in the case was on re-canvass the next morning when we interviewed a woman at a nearby house, Lorraine Kolomick, who said she'd been driven to work that morning by her son who lived with her, and that the son had dropped her off around seven A.M. and then brought the car home and then left somewhere with his brother who lived in Rockaway. In other words, she put the son who lived with her and his brother with access to the crime scene if they'd wanted to do something. The woman also said that when she came home that night the son wasn't there and she hadn't seen or heard from him since. We got the dates of birth on both this woman's sons, Michael and Richard, and when we called the Bureau of Criminal Investigation we found out both brothers had rap sheets for narcotics and one had a conviction for burglary.

The mother didn't have Richard's address in Rockaway, all she had was a girlfriend's phone number. We ran that through the Cole's Index and came up with an address on Beach 19th Street, where we went and had the landlady open the apartment.

It was the dirtiest apartment I've seen in all my time on The Job. There was every type of fast-food bags and containers just thrown on the floor. The sink was filled with dirty dishes and dirty water that must have been there for weeks. The one *thing current in that whole apartment was the copy of the* Daily News *from the day before, open to the picture of that woman standing bleeding in the street with her throat cut trying to get help.*

The landlady said the apartment was rented to a Ronnie Testa who worked at a co-op supermarket in Rosedale. We went to this market and talked to Ronnie Testa in the meat department, and she was far from being cooperative, but we did get out of her that her boyfriend Richard lived there with her and sometimes his brother Michael would stay over. That market smelled so bad and this woman did that on the way back we rode with all the windows open in the car.

Since we figured these guys were in the Rockaway area we let all the Rockaway precinct detectives know and also the detectives in Nassau County that these were junkies we were looking at on a potential homicide and any skel who helped us pick them up would get consideration in his or her own situation. The next day we got a call around two in the afternoon from the 4th Squad Nassau County Police that two guys who'd been picked up in a narcotics sweep would give these brothers up if they got a walk on their own arrests. We showed these guys the pictures of the two brothers in an array of other photos and they picked the brothers out and told us where to find them.

I called for the task force, the other homicide detectives who were working the case, and they came down and we circled the house the skels told us about, which was on Mott Street in Rockaway. I looked in, saw these two brothers on the couch and yelled to both of them, and after some back-and-forth they came out.

We brought the two brothers in. I rode with Michael, who'd lived next door to the victim and was the uglier of these two skanky brothers, and while he was in the car he gave it up to me that he never hurt anybody, it was his brother that did it.

Michael said Richard came to his house around eight A.M. after Michael had dropped his mother at work, and Richard said he was sick and needed money to cop and Michael said he was broke. Then Michael said he went into the backyard and watched as Richard broke the basement window of the Farley residence. Michael said he then went back into his own house and a short time later Richard joined him and was very agitated and Michael asked what happened and Richard said, "I put a cord around her neck." And that they then left the house for Rockaway to get drugs.

One thing, when I was questioning Michael, I knew the only thing keeping Kathleen Farley alive was a breathing machine and she was going to die. But neither of these brothers knew that. When I was talking to Michael I said, "You know, this is essentially a burglary that went wrong, the stink here is 'cause of the picture in the newspaper, but the woman's alive and they're taking care of her in the hospital," and so on, minimizing the seriousness of what these guys were looking at, which I think helped get the one shitheel to roll on his brother.

*At the station house I talked to Richard, and he confirmed
what Michael said and explained that he was on acid and
sick needing heroin and that all he could think after he'd broken in and Kathleen Farley had seen him was that she knew
him from when he was growing up and could ID him and that
he was so high he might have cut her but he didn't remember, all he knew was that he'd hurt her, he did remember putting an electrical cord around her neck. So I had him put all
that in his statement.*

In getting ready to meet Bill, I'd read newspaper coverage
of the trial of Richard Kolomick the year following his
arrest. Kolomick's lawyer asked the judge to exclude Kolomick's confession on the ground it had been coerced.
Kolomick himself had taken the stand and testified that
in the station house, in the process of obtaining his statement, Bill had beaten him "for what seemed like an eter-
nity." I mentioned having seen these articles to Bill, who
at first seemed not to take the subject up.

*On our follow-up investigation on these guys, after we'd locked
them up, a couple days later we got another call from the 4th
Squad out in Nassau County, who had given us the initial in-
formants. They said they had gotten word that the Kolomicks
had gotten drugs for some of Kathleen Farley's jewelry from a
male Hispanic known as Tex. We checked records and came
out with a Texadore Ortiz and tracked down where this guy
lived, and when we went there found his girlfriend, whose
name was Evelyn Davila, and after some conversation she
agreed to meet us a little while later at the Beach 25th Street*

subway station with certain items she knew had been stolen. We met her there and she produced the jewelry her drug-dealer boyfriend had received in exchange for some heroin. Through Evelyn Davila we got to the woman, Nora Mercado, who'd traded the jewelry for the heroin, and she admitted she'd purchased the jewelry from Richard Kolomick earlier that week for twenty dollars. I took the jewelry to Joseph Farley and he identified it as being his wife's. This was four hours before they took Kathleen Farley off life support and she died.

I also reinterviewed Ronnie Testa after Richard had given it up, and she stated that the day I spoke to her at the meat market, she found Richie at Frankie's, which was the Mott Street house where we picked Richard and Michael up, and she told Richard we'd been to see her at the meat market, and he became nervous and stated he couldn't believe he did it, he said he went crazy, he was on acid and he'd strangled the woman in the house near where he'd lived. I met this Ronnie Testa's aunt several years later and she told me her niece still went to see Richard in prison, she was always getting stopped and cavity-searched by the guards, who thought she was smuggling in heroin. A few years after that they found her dead on Rockaway Beach.

I realized that in a roundabout way Bill was trying to respond to my question about Kolomick's allegations.

"These two brothers killed this woman. You understand that, don't you?"

"Right, I understand," I said.

"They did it. Now, has it ever happened a cop laid hands on a guy to get him on record telling the truth? Where a guy is guilty and the cop knows it—he's got witnesses like this skel's brother who've told him what happened but who might not stand up in court or even be around, and the cop knows a confession is the only evidence that doesn't go away, or that some smart-ass lawyer can't turn upside down—has it ever happened a cop laid hands on a guy to get him to tell the truth? Yeah, that's happened.

"Did I beat Richard Kolomick?" Bill looked me in the eye. "No," he said. "I didn't beat him."

WHEN BILL WAS GROWING up in Brooklyn, one of his jobs after school was to take care of his father's mother, who lived down the street with Bill's aunt. Bill's grandmother was a Ukrainian immigrant who spoke little English and was diabetic and by this point in her life almost a complete invalid. His aunt worked for the phone company from four in the afternoon to midnight, and it was Bill's responsibility after school to go to his grandmother's house, prepare her dinner, then take care of her animals—the pigeons, rabbits, and chickens that she raised for food.

After his chores, Bill would sit with his grandmother and change channels on the television for her until it was time to serve her dinner. This was 1954; Bill's grandmother had a small black-and-white set, and she particularly liked the westerns. Her favorites were Hop-along Cassidy, Gene Autry, and Roy Rogers. As I've said, she didn't speak any English, but Bill remembers that she had a lovely smile and he enjoyed the hours he'd sit with her.

This picture of Bill when he was eight years old taking care of his grandmother's animals and then keeping company with the old woman into the dinner hour is a key to his nature. Bill is a violent man, and his whole adult life has been spent comfortably among violent men. But he also has a gentleness, decency, and sweetness of spirit that ground and qualify the violence of his life. I've seen Bill spend long minutes scratching the head of one of the dozens of birds he breeds and raises, listened to his worries about the skin condition of his dog, watched the patience with which he taught my boy Ben to ride a bicycle when health problems prevented me from doing that, or how Bill turned away, concealing tears of happiness and pride when he received a loving note from one of his daughters at Christmas. This is the person about whom the story circulates that, when confronting a skel who had just shot a cop and was concealing the whereabouts of another perpetrator, Bill drove his thumb into the skel's open shoulder wound—the skel having been shot while fleeing—grinding bullet against bone until the skel gave up where the other perpetrator was hiding.

We did a story suggested by the Kathleen Farley case in the first script I wrote after Bill and I met. Kelly and Sipowicz interview the perpetrators, whom we call the Delio brothers, and neither brother is beaten to get a statement, which was how Bill told me the story. I didn't write a script about suspects getting beaten until four shows later, when everyone knew each other better.

Bill at the scene of a homicide

chapter 2

Getting involved with *NYPD Blue* brought big changes to Bill's life, the most immediate and dramatic of which had to do with money. When Bill was twelve and working for a florist it had seemed natural to him to walk two and a half miles from the flower shop to a mortuary carrying a five-foot-high, twenty-five-pound burial wreath because he'd left the school pass at home which would have saved him five cents on the bus. His take-home pay as a detective had never been more than six hundred dollars a week, and the moonlighting jobs he'd work might bring in another two or three hundred. Now he'd been paid $5,000 to do three or four hours' worth of reading and give comments on two sixty-page scripts. Bill told me later that he'd felt as if he was stealing.

I knew that after twenty-five years on The Job Bill was hoping to work out a way to support himself after his retirement, so I made sure he understood that while the money was good and might get a lot better, the odds against success in what we were doing were high. For every series that became a hit, I told him twenty failed, especially hour dramas, which in that year were regarded by the deep thinkers in network programming as costly relics of a time before the attention span of the viewing public had been irreversibly shortened by sound bites and MTV.

The show's prospects were further affected by the diminished power of my boss and mentor and colleague Steven Bochco, who no longer had the leverage that had come from hits like *Hill Street Blues* and *L.A. Law*—series that generated huge profits for the network in advertising revenues and also created the audience allegiance that allowed shows in neighboring time slots to develop and become successful and make the network even more money. Steven's precedent-setting ten-series deal at ABC had produced *Doogie Howser,* no more than a moderate success, and also ratings failures like *Capital Critters* and *Cop Rock. Civil Wars,* his only series then on ABC's schedule, had received respectable reviews but was a ratings disappointment, and, like all of Steven's shows, was tremendously expensive for the network to air because of the generous terms of his contract.

Given whatever disenchantment with Steven ABC may have been feeling, and the prevailing wisdom of advertisers that the hour drama was headed for extinction—not to mention misgivings then being trumpeted on op-ed pages and in Senate subcommittees about the unhealthy effects on young people of television's mediocrity and its casually incessant portrayal of violence—the timing of Steven's insistence that *NYPD Blue* break new ground in terms of language and nudity on network television couldn't have been worse. ABC said it would schedule *NYPD Blue* if the parties could work out exactly what expansions of language and how much nudity would be involved, but as his negotiations dragged on with the network's Department of Standards and Practices, Steven sometimes expressed doubt to me that coming to an agreement was what the other side had in mind.

Still, in these first three or four months of our knowing each other, Bill's uncertainties had more to do with my work habits than with the show's precarious prospects. I own and bet on Thoroughbreds, and our conversations about future scripts tended to take place while I was following the fortunes of one or another of my horses. This didn't help Bill's sense of the long-term promise and stability of our collaboration.

After our talks that spring in Manhattan, we got together next in July, in Las Vegas, where the casinos were carrying a closed-circuit telecast of a $200,000 stake in New Jersey in which a two-year-old colt I owned was running. I'd flown in from Los Angeles to watch the race and had sent Bill a ticket to come out from New York. Bill loves to travel— getting to see new parts of the country was what he'd most enjoyed when he'd moonlighted as a bodyguard for clients like Steve Ross, the CEO of Time Warner. Surprisingly, none of these jobs had ever taken him to Nevada.

The horse whose race we'd come to see was named Gilded Time. I'd bought the colt at an auction in Florida, and he'd won his first start three weeks before at Hollywood Park in Los Angeles. Although in that race he'd been running against ordinary competition, his performance had been impressive because, when the starting gate opened, he had stood gawking at the other horses and spotted the field fifteen lengths, a next-to-impossible margin to overcome in a six-furlong sprint. Gary Stevens, his jockey, explained later that, after this beginning, his goal had been to try to get the horse some education—if he could get close enough to the pack, Gilded Time would get dirt in his face and experience what racing was like.

By the far turn, Gilded Time had caught the next-to-last horse and was making ground up so fast Stevens steered him to the middle of the track to keep from running up on other horses' heels. Running wide in this fashion added a hundred yards to the distance they had to cover. Still, by the head of the stretch they'd circled the pack and gained the lead—Gilded Time was drawing away, cocking his ears and turning his head to peer toward the grandstand, where people were shouting in excitement and surprise.

I've followed horse racing since I was a boy. My dad was a surgeon who owned a few inexpensive claiming horses, and my strongest memories from childhood come from the week we'd get to spend together in August at the track in Saratoga. When I changed jobs, going from university teaching to working on *Hill Street*, I got involved in owning horses myself. The first script I wrote won the Emmy and the Writers Guild Award and also a cash award called the Humanitas Prize given by the Catholic Church. I used this money to buy into a horse called Evening M'Lord. Over the next ten years I bought and campaigned more horses, a few of which won big races, although on balance they'd cost me a lot more than I made.

From the morning he'd first seen Gilded Time working out in Florida, my trainer, Darrell Vienna, had said he thought the horse might be a champion. After this first race in California we decided to enter the stake in New Jersey called the Sapling, which was the first big race of the year in America for two-year-olds. Because Gilded Time hadn't originally been nominated I had to put up an extra $12,500 to get him in. It cost another $20,000 to fly the horse and a groom and his jockey across country. If he won, the owner's share would be $96,000. A three-to-one return on the money it would cost to run was taking lousy odds, but I wanted to find out what kind of horse I had.

Bill later told me that when he showed up at the Mirage Hotel with his notes on the first two scripts, he brought a lot of doubts with him. Even if it was a city he'd always wanted to see, for us to meet in Las Vegas so I could watch a horse race put our working together in a light of unreality. But Bill kept his reservations to himself. Instead, we talked about what he called the Case of the Dove.

It was the night before Gilded Time's race, after we'd had our regulation steak dinner, and I'd walked Bill around the various gaming tables. The only bets he made were on the Wheel of Fortune. He bet $10, taking two-to-one odds, that the $2 bill would come up on the wheel, and on the first roll he won. Then he lost twice. When the wheel came up wrong the second time Bill stared at the wheel man. I thought he was going to punch him in the nose.

That ended the gambling for the night. I didn't want to gamble, because once I start I tend not to stop or pay much attention to what else is going on, and I didn't want to be ignoring Bill. We walked outside. Even at night it was eighty-five degrees.

This was an eleven-year-old boy who disappeared at around three P.M. one afternoon. His parents notified the police in the early evening. Uniform cops searched for the boy all through the night, and I caught the case in the morning when the boy was officially declared missing. I remember, after I'd talked to the parents, who were an immigrant couple from East Europe, after I saw the apartment they lived in and they'd told me about their son, I knew something bad had happened to him, because this boy hadn't run away, there was too much love for him where he lived.

I called for Aviation and Emergency Services so we could intensify the search. It was in an area of Queens called College

Point, and because of the proximity to the water, I also had Harbor in. Sergeant Auerbach, I remember, was the uniform sergeant, a real nice guy. He told me one of the uniform cops had said that two kids in the area had seen the missing boy, whose name was Chris Keszegh, with a guy named Freddy that previous afternoon. I had them take me to where they said Freddy lived. When I got to Freddy's house, he had been sleeping, he said, but he smelled of alcohol. I asked him if he had seen the kid the day before, and he said, "Yeah, I saw him in the park but then he left."

The standard question I ask anybody who possibly looks wacky is "When's the last time you were in the hospital?" For some reason that makes them feel you've got power over them, like you can see in their heads. This Freddy, whose last name was Faeth, when I asked him when he was in the hospital last he looked at me as if I knew the answer and said, "Two years ago." I said, "What were you in there for?" He says, "Well, I jumped off a roof, trying to kill myself." I said, "All right, Freddy, why don't you put some clothes on, you come with me and help me look for this kid, you know what the kid looks like."

So he got dressed and he came with me, and when I got up to where the search was being conducted, there was another kid who came up and said that him and another guy had been with Freddy in the park the day before when Freddy was drinking beer, and they had chased Chris Keszegh away, he was a young kid and they wanted to drink beer with Freddy. So at this point we had someone saying Freddy wasn't the last guy to see Chris, but I still liked him for the perpetrator and wanted to keep my hands on him. I took him back to the station house and put him with an old-time detective there named Gene Kelly. I said, "Gene, just do me a favor, just keep him here so that he doesn't go. Under any circumstances, don't let him leave." I told Freddy that he was there, again, to assist us in looking for this child.

At that point, I got a call over the radio that Emergency Services wanted me at a spot in the lot, and I immediately knew that they had found the boy. I guess up to that point, I still kind of hoped that he was alive. When I got there, he was in the weeds next to an abandoned step-van in this vacant lot. An Emergency Services guy, in walking around there, had stepped on the body. I remember looking down on the boy's body. Some bees were crawling up his nose and I shooed them away. I saw strangulation marks around the throat. I looked up from where he was laying and saw that you could see his house from where he was laying dead.

I went back to the boy's house to tell his father and mother. I took the father into the bedroom. There was nobody there for this guy. I said there was no easy way for me to tell him what I had to say. He just leaned over onto me and I held him while he cried. I asked him if he wanted me to tell his wife, and he said, "No," but at that time she actually looked into the room and saw what was going on so she knew.

I went back to the precinct and looked into Freddy more. He was a chronic alcoholic, had been treated in a bunch of programs. Six months previous to him jumping off the four-story building two years before, the police department had pulled him off a roof where he was clinging to the gutter of a six-story building. Plus, he'd been questioned five years before in the murder of a sixteen-year-old boy, which was a case that never got solved.

This was a weekend, a Saturday morning. The neighbors had already started circulating leaflets, of which I have one, of pictures of Chris. The press was down there, so the Inspector had called. I was briefing him on what I had and also briefing the homicide task force which was working the case. With finding out about this guy Freddy Faeth's background, I was ninety-five percent sure I had the right guy in custody. I told a couple of task force guys that if they wanted to go in and start on him, or just interview him, I said, "You know, this is the guy, I'm sure he's going to fold." They went in and ten minutes later they came out and said he had confessed. I went in and took the whole statement. I polished up his initial statement a little bit.

The next morning, I had to take someone from the family to the morgue to make an identification. When I got to their residence the grandmother was there. Whether or not she was from the father's or mother's side, I don't know. She was a big woman. European. She said she was going to come with me. I took her to the morgue. When they opened the blinds on the viewing glass she kept patting one hand against the window like you'd pat a child's face to make him feel better.

After the ID the Medical Examiner took me to one side. Freddy had said that he had orally sodomized the boy and then strangled him because he was afraid the boy would tell on him, but the Medical Examiner said besides being strangled the boy had been anally sodomized, his face had been pushed into the ground while he was being raped, and he also had some marks on the top of his chest and she didn't know what they were and she wanted me to take a look.

I told the doctor, "Listen, you don't have to show me the whole body. I could do without seeing that." She said, "Well, I'd like your idea on this." She took me into the autopsy room, and the dead boy was wrapped up in white plastic and tape. She ripped this tape off and this white plastic. What they do in autopsies, they open up the chest cavity and trunk, and he was sewn up with these big stitches, and in the plastic was all this blood-and-water mixture. The mark on his chest was where he had been held up against the step-van, the front grill of the step-van, and I told her that's what it was.

I was mad at the ME for making me look at the whole body. I hated thinking of the boy being hurt like this and dying within sight of his own home and how when this Freddy Faeth had jumped off the building doctors working for the city had helped him and when he was hanging from the gutter my department had helped him, and now this kid was dead. I had seen lots of dead bodies in my life, but this one, to see it like that, unnecessarily, really made me mad at that Medical Examiner.

The next day, I had to pick up the family for the Grand Jury. I think it was just the father and grandmother again. When I got to the house, before we left, the grandmother took me outside. It was a two-story brick house, and on the edge of the roof she pointed out a white dove. A white pigeon. She said, "It came yesterday, and it's been here ever since. It is a sign for us that Chris is in heaven. This dove is here looking after us." I'm an old pigeon flier, and I could not figure out, for the life of me, why that pigeon was there. That type of bird just doesn't do that sort of thing. A white pigeon. I was glad the family had that to believe in.

We'd been walking along the Strip and had come to an undeveloped lot between the hotels, which was just sand and scrub grass and refuse. I told Bill the story of the dove was one we'd definitely want to use (and we did, in the seventh episode of our first season). After a moment Bill asked, "What do you think of this horse?" I told him we'd know a lot more in twenty-four hours. "But you believe in him?" he asked. I told Bill I thought he might be a great horse. "Yeah, well, I hope it works out for you," Bill said.

THE NEXT DAY GILDED Time won his race—no two-year-old in the world ever ran six furlongs as fast as he did that afternoon. Bill bet on the race and won $200. He kept saying he was amazed, and that he was happy for me, he couldn't believe something like this could ever work out.

First season cast of *NYPD Blue*. (David Caruso declined to allow his photographs from the show to be included in this book.) *Used by permission of Capital Cities/ABC, Inc.*

chapter 3

Finally, in late fall, Steven and ABC worked out a framework for resolving their impasse that allowed the preproduction process to begin. The decision on how much nudity was acceptable was postponed until after filming. On the issue of language, the parties would work to establish a pool of permissible profanities and a limit to how many times in aggregate these could be heard in an episode —the when and where of their use would be Steven's to choose. Steven joked that the March Hare from *Alice in Wonderland* had come to him in a dream with the idea for this compromise.

The plan was to shoot the first two episodes on a single twenty-day schedule. Sets would be built in Los Angeles at Twentieth Century–Fox, which distributed Steven's shows, with locations shot in New York. Greg Hoblit, the brilliant producer-director who'd shepherded both *Hill*

Street and *L.A. Law,* was interested in directing these first hours, although because Greg had feature projects in development he was reluctant to commit to staying with the show through the rest of the season.

From the time we began talking about *NYPD Blue,* Steven and I had agreed that Dennis Franz should play Andy Sipowicz, the alcoholic older detective. We'd both worked previously with Dennis on *Hill Street* (in fact, he'd played two different detectives), and on a short-lived series about a minor-league baseball team called *Bay City Blues.* Also, Dennis had starred on a spin-off of *Hill Street* called *Beverly Hills Buntz* which my colleague Jeff Lewis and I had written and which had aired intermittently for a season on NBC. Despite a few misgivings about adding a twenty-seventh cop role to his résumé, Dennis had already signed to play Sipowicz.

Steven's choice for John Kelly was Jimmy Smits, whose career had been launched when they'd worked together on *L.A. Law.* He and Jimmy had begun talking about the role the previous spring, when it appeared *NYPD Blue* would be scheduled in the fall of 1992, and Steven now formally offered the part. But Jimmy, like Greg Hoblit, hesitated to undertake the long-term commitment of doing another series, so Alexa Fogel, head of casting for ABC in New York, and Junie Lowry-Johnson, who casts for Steven in Los Angeles, began drawing up lists of potential Kellys, along with candidates for the other roles.

Meanwhile, in this last week of October, Bill made his first visit to Los Angeles. Bill stayed at our house, where he and my wife, Rita, began a friendship which was a strength for both of them during some difficult times that followed. Our children, Elizabeth, Ben, and Olivia, who then were nine, seven, and four, were awed by Bill's beefy face and frame and taken in like puppies by his gruff overtures. The night he arrived, still on New York time and having worked a double shift before getting on the plane, Bill went to sleep early, and the children took turns going downstairs to hear him snore.

The main reason for Bill's trip was to meet Steven, a prospect that had worried him for a while. I'd made clear that while we carried equal titles as executive producers and creators of *NYPD Blue*, Steven owned the company I worked for—he was my boss. At this point I was paying for Bill's consultancy, but he knew that Steven ultimately would determine his relationship to the show.

When I came downstairs the following morning, Bill was already dressed and sitting in the kitchen. I asked him how he'd slept. "Fair, you know," he said. "Not too bad. Did I snore?" This turned out to be a point of considerable sensitivity for Bill. I told him the children had thought he was being strangled in his room.

Bill was thinking about bosses. After a minute he said, "I had a boss on the .44 Caliber Killer case, Inspector

Dowd. He'd had me transferred out of my squad so I could work for him. I was on that case a year, and finally we grabbed this wacko up, David Berkowitz. The Son of Sam. I figured, any grade promotions come down on this case, I gotta be part of. Didn't happen."

Michael Daly had told me about the aftermath of the Son of Sam arrest, how it was considered a disgrace among the detectives who'd worked the case that Bill hadn't gotten promoted.

"I worked for another lieutenant, Joe Perillo, Joe the Boss they called him. Hated the Irish. The worst thing ever happened to this guy was seeing *Kojak*. Perillo was always butting into how his detectives worked a case."

I told Bill one of Steven's strengths was knowing what work people were capable of and letting them do it.

That detective Gene Kelly, helped me collar Freddy Faeth? Gene had thirty years on the job, and this Perillo once screamed at him for ten minutes in front of a whole squad, humiliated him, 'cause Gene tried to throw someone a break.

A cop who's doing his job isn't just looking to lock up bad people. People who are basically all right, where either by their own mistake or being in the wrong place at the wrong time they're jammed up, a good cop tries to get these people through their problem, which was all Gene was doing.

This Perillo, with his miserable disposition, he was always looking to do the opposite. Once I caught a case, a real stinky
one, a kid had got beat up by four guys outside a bar, and
this kid's father was a cop, and when the kid came home afterward and his father found out what happened the father
takes the kid back out on the street outside the bar and holds
his off-duty gun on the other three guys while his son and the
guy who originally started the trouble with him had a fair fight.
Now later in the night there's a fire under this cop's car, then
later there's damage to the tires on one of the guy's cars who
was watching the fight, and by the time I catch the case I'm
up to my hips in cross-complaints.

So I'm trying to straighten this thing out, I bring all these kids
and their parents into the squad, and I'm letting them know if
anybody gets locked up everybody gets locked up, the judge
can figure out who did what. Basically, I'm looking to cool the
thing out and keep everyone out of court, and I've got it pretty
much squared away, and now here comes my boss mouthing
off, "these Irish drunks," this and that. Notifies Internal Affairs,
because a cop's involved, and I gotta go through a whole
other round of interviews with Internal Affairs looking over my
shoulder before I can quiet things down again.

Another time some furniture delivery guy unloads at this furniture warehouse and the guy who's supposed to sign for it says
something's wrong with the load and he won't sign, and the
delivery guy says take the complaint up with the company,
he's gotta get a signature. So then allegedly the warehouse

guy pulls a gun on the delivery guy and tells him get the hell off the property.

The delivery guy comes into the station house bringing charges on the warehouse guy for brandishing the weapon, and I bring the warehouse guy in and I've got it just about straightened out where the delivery guy gets a signature for his load and the rest of it goes away, but this miserable Perillo, because the dad of the warehouse guy who supposedly pulled the gun is friends with the captain downstairs, Perillo tells me fill out separate interview forms on every witness and let the DA decide whether to prosecute, we don't want to play favorites. I say, "Boss, the driver just wants a signature for his load and this whole thing stays out of court," but Perillo starts yelling I don't get to shit-can a case on his watch and maybe Internal Affairs should look at how friendly the captain downstairs is with the guy who owns this furniture warehouse and how friendly is the guy with me.

The last straw, he wanted me to lock up a cop who'd gotten into a fender-bender where no one was hurt at all but there was a discrepancy in statements if the cop's girlfriend was driving or him. Here's a situation with no victim and no reason to pursue the case, but this Perillo makes the cop turn his gun in and his shield, the guy's in the squad room crying, twelve years on the job, and I told the boss, bullshit, I wasn't gonna sign the papers, someone else could sign the paperwork on the case. After that I put in for transfer, but thank God the boss got transferred before I did.

Bill looked over at me, having made himself miserable. "Bill," I said, "my boss isn't like that."

WE HAD LUNCH WITH Steven at an Italian restaurant near the studio. Because the subject was already on Bill's mind and I thought it would show how Bill's anecdotes could bring alive the workings of the squad, I encouraged him to talk about Perillo's relations with his detectives.

Once this boss broke such balls at a murder scene the Crime Scene Unit guys didn't lift a single print, which was an impossibility at that scene, but that's how much they hated this guy.

I got in touch with a doctor at the ME's Office and got him to come back out with an assistant to reprocess the crime scene, and they took some blood samples which wound up being helpful down the road, plus they lifted a pubic hair from a male black off the woman's body who'd been murdered, which helped on the follow-up investigation giving us an idea who we were looking for.

This woman, Elisa Kamenoff, had a kitchen knife in her chest. She'd been raped and stabbed, and she had bite marks in her genital area. There was a trail of blood leading from the window outside her apartment across the garage roof and through a playground and over a fence on another street, and on a rooftop on that street there was another break-in at an-

other apartment. The woman who lived in that apartment was lucky she was out of town that night.

We got nowhere on that case for a long time. Then a married couple in their eighties was murdered during a home invasion in another area of the borough, Richmond Hill. They were found in the basement of their residence, where the man used to make these cement planters, bowls that he used for planters in a garden, they were tied up down there and the husband was actually skinned alive and the woman had died of multiple knife wounds. This couple, the Albergas, had two sons, both in their late forties, and one of the sons had a boy who was a drug addict, and the other grown son was sure the drug-addict nephew was involved with doing away with this elderly couple, and so the tragedy caused by this incident went on and on tearing that family up.

All we could get from the Alberga crime scene was a palm print. Three days later, a few doors down, some black guys came in through a back window and they tied up another family and ransacked their house, but then they heard a neighbor pulling in and they ran. So what we had, by the family that was tied up describing these black guys and the similarity of that break-in to this vicious murder three doors down, and how that murder had some similarities with the Elisa Kamenoff homicide, tentatively we put these crimes in a pattern as being committed by the same perpetrators.

Finally, six weeks after that in Whitestone, Queens, three male blacks entered a house through a back window and pro-

ceeded to take a kitchen knife, consistent with the other cases, woke up the husband and wife and tied them up with neckties, marched the fourteen-year-old son down to the master bedroom and beat him unconscious, beat the husband, and a twenty-one-year-old daughter was raped.

The next night a guy walks into the 75th Precinct in East New York, Brooklyn, and says he was driving the getaway car for some guys in a robbery in Queens and when the guys got back in the car they were talking about a girl being raped. This guy, whose name was Willie Blount, said he was mad that the other guys did a rape when it was only supposed to be a robbery and he wanted to give these guys up.

Chris Dowdell and I were investigating the Whitestone home invasion. Chris went to the 75th Precinct station house to interview Willie Blount, then called me at the bar where I was working as a bouncer (we were both off-duty) and said I should meet him.

We figured what might've happened is Willie decided his license plate could have been made when they were pulling away or maybe these guys beat him on the count for what they'd robbed and he was pissed off. Anyway, when we searched his car we found under the backseat a kitchen knife which was the same type knife used on the family in Whitestone (Chris had taken a knife from the Whitestone house to have available for comparison). It was also the same type I found sticking out of Elisa Kamenoff.

Willie Blount indicated the guys who did the home invasion were his nephew, Eris Blount, another guy named Daniel Hayes, and another guy, McNeil. He gave us a house to set up on in Bedford-Stuyvesant, in Brooklyn. We set up a couple of cars and a van on this snowy night. Somebody called in a phony ten-thirteen—assist an officer—on us, and we knew in a matter of time everybody in that area was going to be aware we were out there, so we went into the building to snatch these guys out.

We hit the first floor apartment and we got Daniel Hayes right away. We hit the second floor, where some old woman was on the toilet bowl. The next floor up, we got Eris Blount.

We brought these guys Eris Blount and Daniel Hayes into the house, and after a couple hours, they both admitted to the case in Whitestone. Both of them laid the rape off on the missing guy, McNeil.

We hit McNeil's house and came up empty. Every place we went looking for this guy we carried shotguns to make him know we were prepared to do what we had to do to get him in. He surrendered himself a little while later. I remember we had him handcuffed behind his back and he complained he had an itchy nose that was driving him crazy. I looked at this guy who had committed all these sick crimes, and here he is worried that he couldn't itch his nose.

Because of the similarity of the crimes, we took palm prints which would be compared against the print in the case of the

Albergas. We also had a lineup to see if the family from Whitestone could identify these guys, and the daughter picked out
Eris Blount as the rapist.

This Eris Blount also had odd teeth, and their spacing
matched the bite marks on the first victim, Elisa Kamenoff. I
got a court order to draw blood from Blount to compare with
the blood we'd picked up when the ME went back to the Kamenoff apartment. In that situation, if the suspect makes any
form of declination you can't take the sample unless the court
authorizes necessary force, which in this case the judge had
done, so when I took Eris Blount to the emergency room at
Elmhurst General I told him either he could let the doctor
draw his blood or if he wouldn't cooperate we could scrape
his blood off the floor.

The blood came up a match. Also the palm prints were a
match from the Alberga case. Blount, Hayes, and McNeil
went to trial on the Whitestone case and got convicted there.
On the Alberga case we also got convictions. Eris Blount got
so much time on these two we never went to bat on the Elisa
Kamenoff case.

We know he did a lot of others too. For example, I got a call
from a girl named Goldstein who said that in 1975 she was
being raped in the same apartment complex where Elisa Kamenoff got murdered, a few doors down, when an off-duty
cop heard her screaming and came to the stairwell where she
was and saved her. She ID'd Eris Blount and he was brought
in, but because he was a juvenile he served almost no time at

all. In looking at his juvenile record he had been arrested twelve times, just about nothing done to him.

I remember at the hospital that day when we were getting his blood sample this guy threatened me, something to the effect someday he was going to get me. I let him know what I thought of him at that point. The nerve of this guy, to threaten me at that point, after all we knew he did. It took four guys from the task force and the doctor to get me off him.

WHEN WE WERE LEAVING the restaurant after lunch, Steven held me back a step so Bill couldn't hear us. "Do not let this guy out of your sight," he said.

New York City welcomes the *NYPD Blue* cast with open arms—here David Caruso and Bill are on location. This photo appeared on the front page of the second section of *The New York Times*. *Used by permission of* The New York Times

chapter 4

The production began to come together. Bill was hired as *NYPD Blue*'s technical adviser, which of course only began to describe his contribution to the show. As well as directing a number of episodes, Greg Hoblit would produce the series for the entirety of the first season, which assured continuity in the look and feel of the film. Paul Eads signed on as production designer and began making the rounds of precinct station houses in New York to gather impressions for the set we'd build in Los Angeles. (Paul would win an Emmy for his work.)

By mid-February, Alexa Fogel and Junie Lowry-Johnson had cast about half the roles. In New York, Nicky Turturro was signed to play the naive James Martinez and Amy Brenneman to play Licalsi, the uniform cop who is blackmailed into informing on John Kelly. James McDaniel, with whom Steven first worked on the ill-fated

Cop Rock, would portray the boss of the 15th Detective Squad, Arthur Fancy.

Although we were seeing actresses for the role of Laura, Kelly's estranged wife, we felt it was better to defer any decisions until we knew who was playing Kelly, so that Kelly and Laura would be well matched physically. As for our troubles casting Kelly, these weren't unexpected. It's an axiom in television that the male lead is the most difficult series role to fill—actors in their late thirties who are talented, appealing, and available are rare commodities.

By this time I'd completed the third and was at work on the fourth of our scripts. I've mentioned that the Kathleen Farley case inspired the main story in show three. The story line for Sipowicz in our fourth episode was suggested by a case Bill worked in which the original arrest, because of ineffective police work, sent the wrong man to jail.

This was a triple homicide in a liquor store. A couple witnesses described the perp being white, between fifty and sixty. There aren't that many guys in this category, and in being shown mug shots of guys who fit the description, one of the witnesses picked out a parolee by the name of Gergel.

I wasn't on the case, I was working another homicide that came in earlier in the day, but later on in looking at the DD

Fives, which are the reports of the interviews, I saw that several witnesses described the perp in these liquor-store homicides as being six feet two inches. In my experience, whenever they describe a guy being that tall he's at least over six feet or else they describe him as average. This Gergel was five foot eight, plus he had no ties at all to the area in Queens where this liquor store was robbed. To get to that area from Brooklyn, where he lived, he'd've had to make three subway changes.

The guys on the case sat on Gergel's house, and at first one of the detectives walked right past him as Gergel was coming up to the residence, not recognizing him 'cause he was looking for a bigger guy. Then they realized it was Gergel and grabbed him up and brought him from Brooklyn to Queens and he was put in a lineup. One of the guys in that lineup weighed about two hundred and seventy-five pounds. It was a lousy lineup in general. Anyway, one of the witnesses picked Gergel, two didn't, but he had a record for the right kind of crimes, stickups at liquor stores, and he was charged with this triple homicide.

It rubbed me the wrong way about this discrepancy between Gergel's height and the witnesses' first description. I was worried we had the wrong guy, although I have to say this Gergel had a lousy personality, always giving everyone lip.

Anyway, they put Gergel in the system. About a month later a letter came to the squad saying Gergel's not the guy that did it, the actual perp is a guy named Condon, who also had a record and turned out was six foot three and had a sister lived two blocks away from the liquor store where the stickup was pulled.

The guys who caught the case wouldn't buy it could've been Condon. They said Gergel and Condon were both career crimi- nals and their paths had crossed in prison and this is where they said the story about Condon came from, that Gergel knew about Condon's record and had put an informant up to lying about Condon.

When you're not the catching detective on a case, unless your opinion's asked it's not really your place to kibitz too much, especially in a situation like this where they've made an arrest. Even so, bigmouth that I am, I agitated these guys at least to look into Condon. It ate away at me. It got where I started leaving little notes on this one detective's desk—"How'd you like dinner tonight? Gergel ate prison food."

Finally they got a warrant for Condon's apartment in Sunny- side and recovered a bullet from the wall there that matched the bullets recovered from the DOAs at the liquor store. Con- don had been drunk before he pulled the job and fired into the wall. It turned out someone in the building remembered hearing the gunshot that night, which was how they came to look for the bullet. Also in the apartment they recovered a re- ceipt from a magic store for purchase of a fake mustache, which had been a big point for arresting Gergel, that Gergel had a mustache and Condon didn't. At that point Condon got

collared and Gergel was released, and later on Condon was
convicted for these homicides.

In the script for show four, I gave the name Howard Cole-
man to the character based on Gergel. The detective who
resists admitting he's made a wrong arrest is called
Walker. After the emphasis we'd given in our first three
shows to Sipowicz's chaotic personal life, I always felt the
doggedness Andy shows in pursuing his investigation in
this case went a long way toward establishing his effective-
ness and honorable nature as a cop.

Bill had told me Gergel's story during one of the four
or five phone conversations we'd now have every day while
he was working cases in New York and I was writing in
Los Angeles. Later that night he called me back, having
remembered an additional detail.

I guess you can't use this, but after they let him out of Rikers I
saw this lippy little Gergel on the street, and the guy still told
me to go fuck myself, so at least he was consistent.

DAVID CARUSO FIRST AUDITIONED for the role of Kelly in
January, and I didn't like his performance. The audition
scene, taken from the first episode, shows Kelly confronting Sipowicz in a bar about Sipowicz's drinking. David

kept jumping on the end of the speeches of the person reading Sipowicz's part, giving the impression Kelly already knew and had discounted what Sipowicz was about to say. It was a credible but ungenerous interpretation of Kelly's personality.

Steven wasn't present at this original audition, but he was familiar with David's work. He'd cast David on *Hill Street* in a small recurring role as leader of an Irish street gang called the Shamrocks, and earlier in a pilot he'd produced at MTM which hadn't sold.

As the start date for the shoot approached, David's agent sent Steven a reel of his recent work. Steven was taken with David's portrayal of a city detective in Abel Ferrara's film *The King of New York*. He suggested David be reread.

Greg Hoblit, Steven, and I were all present for this second audition, during which David softened and warmed his performance. Steven felt David was right for Kelly, Greg was on the fence, and I remained dug in against. I was concerned that David's original interpretation was an indication of choices he'd make on the set, that Caruso-as-Kelly would emerge a distant and selfish character.

Ultimately, David was among three actors we screen-tested for the lead. We also tested two actresses to play

Laura, finally choosing Sherry Stringfield for Kelly's ex-wife.

As we were making our decision about Kelly, Bill called from New York, saying he'd just seen a movie called *Mad Dog and Glory* in which a redheaded actor named Caruso in one of the supporting roles was 100 percent believable as a cop. Our Los Angeles casting director, Junie Lowry-Johnson, had also suggested I see this film. Finally I did, and wised up.

In retrospect, David seems the inevitable choice for Kelly. I had misgivings about him as a person, and amateurishly confused my reaction at that level with my estimate of his professional craft. Over time my misgivings turned out not to be unfounded, but that doesn't qualify the extraordinary humanity and vividness David brought to his performance of the part.

JUST BEFORE SHOOTING BEGAN, Bill took a week's vacation time to come to Los Angeles, supervise the dressing of the station-house set, and be available to advise the actors on technical aspects of their performance.

He quickly developed an easygoing working relationship with Dennis Franz, whom Bill described as "a knock-around type of guy." This is Bill's top category. Jimmy

McDaniel and Nick Turturro both sought out Bill's opinion and advice and got along well with him.

David kept his distance from Bill. He told me he already knew who Kelly was and didn't want his reactions to Bill's behavior or personality to leak into his interpretation.

Bill respected David's attitude as part of his process as an actor. He wanted to like David. He knew how much the show's chances for success depended on David's work. But David rubbed him the wrong way.

David had grown up in Forest Hills in a neighborhood which was part of the 112th Precinct, where the Queens Homicide Squad is located. During their first conversation, David recalled for Bill that as a teenager he'd made $25 per appearance as a filler in lineups at the precinct station house. Afterward, as we drove home, Bill kept clearing his throat in nervous irritation. "It doesn't matter. What difference does it make? You know, but no filler in the history of that precinct ever got more than five dollars to stand a lineup. Maybe if a guy had to stick around three or four hours you'd throw him an extra pound. That was it, ten dollars maximum."

"Maybe he got the extra money 'cause there weren't a lot of redheads around," I said.

"Bullshit," Bill said.

Bill tried to stay optimistic. "This guy [David] reminds me of a precinct detective I worked with once—a chesty, strutty kind of guy."

There'd been a homicide outside a bar. The DOA was the bartender, a retired cop. He'd been on the street locking up at four in the morning with this old black woman standing next to him who'd been in the bar drinking—when he'd locked up he was gonna walk her to the apartment building where she lived.

A skel with a gun came up to rob them. He grabbed the old woman's purse, then he went for a brown paper bag the bartender was holding which had Chinese food leftovers in it but the skel figured was the night receipts for the bar. The bartender, this retired cop, grabbed at the skel's gun, and the skel shot him and ran off. The retired cop bled to death in the street with this old woman screaming next to him.

The old woman described the perp as white and medium height and having facial hair. A few hours later outside a dive motel a couple blocks away the precinct detectives grabbed up a crackhead couple for questioning 'cause the male, a guy named Kennedy, had a full beard. Kennedy turned out to have multiple arrests for breaking into cars and criminal receiving.

The squad detectives had been talking to this couple in sepa-rate rooms for a couple hours by the time I was called in. In one room Kennedy's crackhead girlfriend was bouncing off the walls, screaming at the top of her lungs with some kind of hallucinations, and the detectives couldn't get any sense out of her. The chesty detective I'm thinking about was named Blasie, and he was in with Kennedy. Blasie liked Kennedy for the homicide and was questioning him pretty aggressively, but Kennedy wasn't giving it up.

I wasn't too comfortable with Kennedy for the perp, because his sheet didn't show him involved with guns at all, especially pulling stickups. Also he had a full-type beard, where the old woman described the perpetrator's facial hair as being scraggly like Redd Foxx had in Sanford and Son.

With Kennedy not giving it up and his girlfriend out of her skull they had to turn this couple loose. Meanwhile I'd been going through Sixty-ones [complaint reports] and found a couple bar stickups in the general area where witnesses described two perps with one of them having a scraggly beard. I said I was going to work the case off this pattern, reinterviewing the witnesses from those other jobs. Blasie said he still liked Kennedy and that's how he was going after it.

You have to understand, it's easy for tension to come up between a homicide detective and the detectives in precinct squads. You walk into their station house, you drink their coffee, you pick up their phones and if it's not about your case you pass the call off to one of them; do that in the wrong tone of voice and it's easy to have the other detective take offense. I always look to be careful about those kinds of things, but in a situation like this, where Blasie was pretty much the fair-haired boy of that squad, more or less being regarded as the top guy, and having the type of attitude he did, which was a belligerent type of attitude and very self-confident, with us having different ideas of the case it didn't matter how careful I was, we weren't going to get along that good. And to tell you the truth, I wasn't in love with this guy and I'm not sure I was that careful with stepping on his toes.

I showed Kennedy's picture to the witnesses in the earlier stickups and no one picked him out. This made me pretty confident I was right not to like him for the robbery-homicide. Also at this time, the old woman's pocketbook turned up floating in the East River where you'd figure it was thrown from a passing car, and this guy Kennedy didn't drive. Even so, Blasie wouldn't back off from saying he was the guy.

I was also working three other homicides, and nothing moved on this case for a month. Then my boss called to tell me the robbery squad had collared a guy with a scraggly beard on an unrelated charge and a witness in one of the other bar robberies had picked the guy out in a lineup.

I went and interviewed this guy, whose name was Richard Calise. After a while Calise gave up a statement on the two other bar stickups, but when I went to work on him for the retired cop, the guy wouldn't go. I gave him every way to do it in terms of not looking at additional time or so forth, but he *said he hadn't done that job. It aggravated me, because I felt like he was telling the truth.*

The next day, Kennedy's whacked-out girlfriend got word to Blasie that Kennedy had confessed to her, and she gave a statement on what he told her with good details in it about the stickup and how he came to have the gun. Off this Blasie picked Kennedy up again. By this time Kennedy was clean-shaven. They ran a lineup where Kennedy and the fillers all wore fake scraggly beards and brought the old lady in from the stickup homicide and she picked Kennedy out. With the old woman's ID and the girlfriend's statement, the DA decided to go to bat. They got an indictment on Kennedy, and I got to build my character congratulating Blasie on the collar.

Kennedy went to trial and they convicted him. Second-degree murder.

"Was he the right guy?" I asked.

"I go over and over that," Bill said. "The thing is, as much as he isn't a likable-type guy with his cocky attitude and so forth, Blasie's a hell of a cop. He'd never've put words in that crackhead girl's mouth." Bill shook his head. "It kills me to admit it, but yeah, I think they got the right guy."

AFTER TWO WEEKS, WE'D completed the Los Angeles part of the shoot. We took a hiatus of several days for the company to move to New York and also to give the producers a chance to view some edited footage and consider mid-course corrections.

Everyone who saw the footage said the work looked great; Greg Hoblit was doing a superb job of directing. The other uniform reaction was that as Kelly, David Caruso was remarkable.

Dennis Franz and Bill pose with Keith Ng,
who was the inspiration for Detective Ng
in the second season.

chapter 5

The company reassembled in Manhattan. We'd caught a great break with weather, which had been mild in the East for several weeks and brought the leaves out early. This meant we wouldn't have to shoot the city defensively, avoiding trees and parks and the like, in order to sell the season as late summer, when the show would premiere.

Bill got us permission to film a series of scenes outside the 9th Precinct station house, on the Lower East Side of Manhattan, which Paul Eads had used as the model for his set. In fact, Bill's friendships with rank-and-file cops and detectives and bosses ranging up to Commissioner Kelly solved or simplified countless production problems. Once *NYPD Blue* went on the air, when we'd film in New York we felt as if the city had adopted us; but already on this first shoot, because of Bill, the cops treated us with hospitality and trust. They were pulling for us.

*   *   *

I HIRED A NUMBER of detectives who were friends of Bill's to work security as we shot. One of these was Bill's last partner, a Chinese detective named Keith Ng.

Keith and I met at the Queens location where we were shooting scenes involving Kelly, Laura, and Laura's neighbor Josh "Four B" Goldstein, who'd been assaulted by a burglar. ("Four B" was played by David Schwimmer, who went on to star in the series *Friends*.)

As we waited for shots to be set up, Bill urged Keith to tell me about some cases he'd worked, which Keith did with the exact mannerisms and intonations of a New York detective, but in speech so heavily Chinese-accented the only words I was sure I understood were obscenities. Every few sentences I'd make out "this fucking guy" or "the fucking guy goes here and picks up" something or other and then there'd be another ten or fifteen seconds of narrative I couldn't follow at all.

Bill was having a great time standing behind Keith watching me try to act as if I understood what Keith was saying. Periodically Bill would interject, straight-faced, "The ransom," or "That's when you went to sit on the house," to reassure Keith that I was tracking his story, and Keith would be off again.

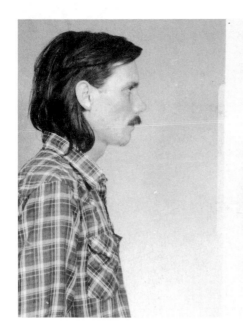

Richard and Michael Kolomick, convicted killers of Kathleen Farley

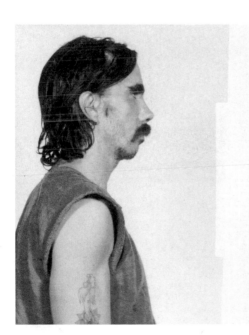

Police come to Kathleen Farley's aid. Photo originally appeared in the New York Daily News.

Bill brings the Kolomick brothers into custody.

The body of eleven-year-old Chris Keszegh was found under the tree next to an abandoned step van. From where he lay, the boy's home can be seen.

Marks from the grill of the van (above) were found on Chris Keszegh's body.

Police photo of Freddy Faeth after he confessed to the killing of Chris Keszegh

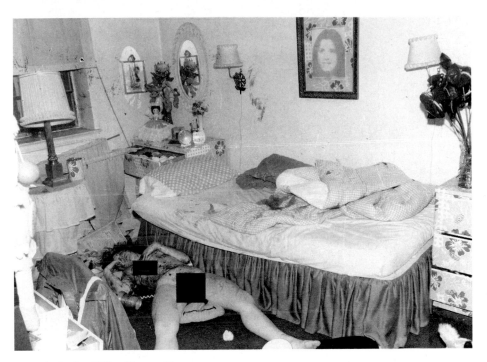

The body of Elisa Kamenoff

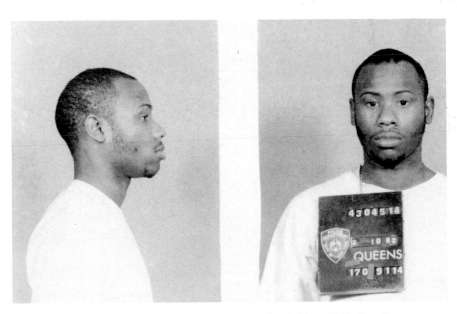

Police photo of Eris Blount, multiple murderer, apprehended by Bill Clark and Chris Dowdell

MISSING PERSON

MPS no 8408/84

PUM no

ANNTONELLA MATTINA : SUBJECT LAST
SEEN AT 1100 HOURS, JULY 16, 1984
LEAVING HER RESIDENCE ENROUTE TO
CITIBANK LOCATED AT CLARSON AND
WILLETS POINT BLVD

DESCRIPTION: FEMALE, WHITE, 12 YEARS
OLD, 5'0", 90LBS. BROWN
HAIR, BROWN EYES, ALSO
WEARS BRACES ON TEETH

CLOTHING: PURPLE JACKET, WHITE BLOUSE
BLUE SHORTS, WHITE SHOES

NY INFORMATION: Contact nearest
Police Officer, or Missing Persons
Squad at Tel.# 374-6913
St. LOMBARDI

Police hoped for a positive response to this flyer.

Police carefully remove the remains of Antonella Mattina.

Police photo of Reginald Harris, aka Flowers, whose confession to a double homicide occurred during Bill's last case on The Job

The body of one of "Flowers's" victims

In fact, Bill was Keith's protector in the Bureau. They'd come to know each other when Keith was a uniform cop in the 5th Precinct. Because he was fluent in three dialects, Keith was loaned to Queens Homicide when Bill was working a series of murders in bowling alleys and restaurants which were frequented by Chinese gangs. Eventually the loan-out became a permanent assignment and Keith received his gold shield.

You have to understand, when I came into the Bureau twenty years before I only had two years on The Job myself. I was fast-tracked because I'd worked undercover, and at the time I came in, guys with a lot of time tended not to trust the new detectives. This was the period of the Knapp Commission investigating police corruption and there was a lot of mistrust, and the more experienced detectives had me sit in cars a lot while they went about their business.

So I knew how it felt being odd man out, and later on when I had some time in the Bureau and seniority, I'd look to take the new guys on, to more or less break them in and show them the ropes, which was the situation with Keith once he was on permanent assignment.

With Keith's language problem he couldn't fill out his DD Fives very well, and the sergeant was always sending them back to be redone. Also, if he had to call BCI for a rap sheet or so forth half the time they'd hang up on him 'cause they figured it was a joke call. So I helped him with his DD Fives and handled most of the phone work.

Keith had lived in this country since he was eleven, but no one in his family and hardly anyone in the neighborhood spoke English. Even in the Marines, where he did a four-year stretch, he was in a Chinese linguists' unit where he was only learning various dialects and not too much English.

Where Keith was gangbusters was an interrogation with one of his own. He was tough, and he got answers, and we wound up clearing a bunch of these cases.

Every detective has strengths and weaknesses. I didn't mind looking out for Keith on his problem areas. The only Chinese expression I knew was "Kung Hai Fat Choi," Happy New Year, which was how I'd say hello to him, but Keith knew I liked him and he was grateful I'd run interference with the sergeant as much as I could.

It happened when he was off-duty Keith worked for some Asian travel agents and promoters who were always organizing bus excursions to Atlantic City for shows put on by big performers they'd brought in from Hong Kong. Keith got me involved with that, initially just in the agency office, where I discouraged some gang guys who'd been coming in and running shakedowns for free tickets, but after a while Keith's boss, Raymond, hired me to work security at the Atlantic City concerts too. I enjoyed having something to do on the holidays when they'd put these shows on, because my wife and I had recently been divorced and special days were a little hard for me. I liked being with these people, they were all good family people.

One thing I feel is people tend to be similar. When I was in Vietnam, one Christmas our infantry unit was in Loc Ninh near the Cambodian border. We'd had a major battle there about a month before, and that Christmas day I remember finding a couple of North Vietnamese bodies outside our base camp where the trenches had collapsed. These bodies had been abused after the battle—certain of our units would leave indications on NV bodies to show that the soldier had been killed by their unit. I dug graves to give these guys a decent burial. I found one guy's wallet and he had pictures of his family and so forth the same as I would, and a library card.

THE MOST IMPORTANT SEQUENCE in the New York shoot shows Kelly struggling to keep Sipowicz out of a suicidal confrontation with mob capo Alfonse Giardella, who'd earlier shot and nearly crippled Sipowicz after Sipowicz had humiliated him in a bar fight. Kelly tries to get Sipowicz to renounce his self-destructive alcoholic fixation on Giardella, in whom Sipowicz sees his own clownishly evil nightmare double.

The Kelly-Sipowicz confrontation was a logistical nightmare too. It begins inside a bar, the Minetta Tavern on McDougal Street, then spills onto the sidewalk and across the street as Kelly strong-arms Sipowicz toward his car. Meanwhile several unmarked police vehicles, summoned by Kelly to protect his partner, arrive and disgorge a group of plainclothes officers, who quickly close on the tavern and place Giardella and several henchmen under arrest.

Bill worked endlessly on the choreography of the sequence with Greg Hoblit, as well as with the actors who would play detectives (Bill's in the scene too, as the detective with the fat red tie). He showed the actors how to move casually past the Giardella soldiers on watch outside the restaurant before turning and taking them by surprise, and how to handle them physically as they are cuffed and taken to the police vehicles. Bill's "dummy" as he demonstrated these arrest techniques was Rob Corn, our assistant director, who came out of the experience bruised and half cross-eyed.

Dennis Franz and David Caruso had difficulties of another sort during rehearsals for the sequence. Dennis was concerned that, rather than locating the scene's emotional line in Kelly's effort to renew Sipowicz's sense of worth, David was portraying Kelly as angrily dismissive, physically manhandling Sipowicz, who, still recovering from his wounds and using a cane, can marshal little resistance.

Possibly David's instincts about how to tone the surrogate father-son relationship between Sipowicz and Kelly were influenced by his own family background. In contrast with Kelly's reverent memories of a father who'd died, killed on duty as a cop when Kelly was eight, David is a child of divorce, and he and his father don't speak.

A time would come, sooner rather than later, when David and Dennis's exchanges on the set were restricted to curt monosyllables about blocking. But on this second-to-the-last day of shooting for the original episodes, through rehearsal after rehearsal they worked together to find a common ground. We had less than an hour and fifteen minutes of daylight remaining when Greg Hoblit printed his first take of the sequence, but by sunset it was done.

ON FILM, KELLY SHOWS a loving generosity as he becomes his teacher's teacher, helping Sipowicz to regain his emotional bearings and rediscover himself as a cop. Kelly watches with pride as Sipowicz exits the car and shouts his resolve to testify against Giardella at trial rather than die with him on the street.

The arrest of Giardella and his soldiers is credible and effective. The first time Bill saw the scene cut together on film, he nodded, looking away. "That looks like a real collar," he said.

ON THE LAST DAY of shooting, Bill brought his dad to the set. We were outside the 9th Precinct station house, and Greg Hoblit invited Walter Clark, who was seventy-nine, to be in the scene as an extra. Greg altered the staging so

that the action began with Bill and his dad walking together into the 9th Precinct station house. Through the
master and two-shots and close-ups, Bill held his dad's
arm and they walked along the sidewalk and entered
through the precinct-house door.

Bill's dad saved the dailies of the various takes of this
scene and played them at night on his VCR.

Outtake from scene between
Andy Sipowitz and Assistant
District Attorney Costas
*Used by permission of Capital
Cities/ABC, Inc.*

chapter 6

The bosses at ABC saw the finished pilot episode on May 17. Bob Iger, who heads the network, and Ted Harbert, president of its Entertainment Division, both reacted with enthusiasm, but let Steven know that their Standards and Practices people had problems with what they'd seen.

A chief offender in the censors' eyes was the conclusion of the pilot's opening sequence. ADA Sylvia Costas (played by Sharon Lawrence), who at this point barely knows Sipowicz, has unenthusiastically walked him through his court testimony as arresting officer in a case Sipowicz has trumped up against Alfonse Giardella. On cross-examination, Sipowicz gets skewered by Giardella's attorney, resulting in the judge's dismissal of the charges. Outside court, Sipowicz accuses Costas of having phoned in her efforts ("You prosecuted the crap out of that one," he says). Costas, making no effort to conceal her contempt, says that she went with the crap she had—i.e., Sipowicz himself. Sipowicz angrily asks if she's accusing him of having lied on the witness stand, and Costas replies that if she thought Sipowicz would understand the term she'd answer "*Res ipsa loquitur*" (Latin for "The thing speaks for itself" or "It's self-evident"). Sipowicz grabs his crotch, saying, "Ipsa this, you pissy little bitch," which was how Standards and Practices got one of their problems.

The censors also objected to a scene in which the shadowed nipple of a woman's breast was unacceptably recognizable, and another, of lovemaking, in which Kelly's downward pelvic thrust was felt to be too emphatic.

It was clear that ABC's tractability in negotiating these issues with Steven would at least partly depend on reaction to the show among prospective advertisers and local station affiliates. The network lost no time testing these waters.

On May 20, at Carnegie Hall, ten minutes of selected footage from *NYPD Blue* was screened for a collection of ad agency executives as part of a presentation promoting the network's fall schedule. The executives' consensus was that the excerpt was exciting and of high quality—and that the network could write off any thought of receiving ad buys from companies or products with a family-oriented image.

On June 3, at the network's annual affiliates' meeting in Los Angeles, the whole of the pilot episode was to be shown to general managers from ABC stations throughout the country. Two days before this meeting, an organization calling itself the American Family Association placed full-page ads in the Sunday supplements of five large-circulation newspapers soliciting signatures (the target figure was two million) for a campaign to combat filth on television as represented by *NYPD Blue*. The campaign's organizer was the Reverend Donald Wildmon of Tupelo, Mississippi. His ads were headlined "This Time TV Has Gone Too Far! We Are FED UP! And We Are Fighting Back." Wildmon's stated goal was to pressure ABC into dropping *NYPD Blue* from its schedule, or, that failing, to organize a boycott of companies that advertised on the show by the two million signers of his petition.

The Wildmon ads were noted by media critics in newspapers throughout the country. Articles about his protest campaign provided a focus for concern among the arriving ABC station managers about the show they were being asked to clear.

The network screened the *NYPD Blue* pilot for the station executives at the Century Plaza Hotel. Afterward, nearly a third of them said they couldn't approve what they had seen for showing in their home markets. A general manager from Alabama said, "You certainly can't fault the quality, but with some of the language and the sex that is in it, we would probably have to preempt." The general manager of a top-ten market affiliate said that *NYPD Blue* was the strongest pilot he'd watched in a number of seasons but that he didn't think network prime time was ready for the show. "Look, I'm from Wichita," said an assistant marketing director for KAKE-TV. "The phone is going to ring off the hook."

Bob Iger was interviewed after the screening and acknowledged that the station executives "are very concerned about the sexual content, about the sexuality. They feel it's gone too far." When he was asked if the version screened for the affiliates would be aired by the network in the fall, he ducked.

The next day, at a follow-up meeting with the affiliates, Dan Burke, CEO of Capital Cities Broadcasting, ABC's corporate parent, described the cut of *NYPD Blue* that had been shown at the Century Plaza as a work in progress. He said one purpose of the screening had been to solicit the affiliates' input before the show's final version was set.

Many journalists covering the meetings were confident they recognized in the ongoing controversy about *NYPD Blue* a craftily calculated effort by Steven to keep the show in the public eye. A few speculated that ABC was colluding in this strategy. No one suggested Reverend Wildmon was in on the con.

In fact, Steven understood that matters were moving in a dangerous direction. If he were to accept ABC's char-

acterization of the pilot as a work in progress and subject
to affiliate "input," he would effectively be abdicating creative control.

In public, Steven kept his reaction to the pilot's being
described as work in progress low-key. ("I have a very
sound and respectful relationship with ABC. I don't expect
for a moment that ABC will put me out on a limb and cut
the limb out from under me.") But he asked for an immediate meeting with Dan Burke, who'd returned to New
York after addressing the affiliates. Burke agreed, and
Steven flew east.

Burke had long found merit in Steven's argument
that hour dramas in the 10:00 P.M. time slot, having
lost viewership to adult-oriented cable programming,
needed to operate on a playing field more nearly level
with cable in terms of language and sexual conventions
if they were to recapture their audience. Although
NYPD Blue caused Burke personal uneasiness (he is an
amiable, straightforward, and religious man who starts
each day by attending mass), he had supported the project's development.

In New York, Burke told Steven he was sorry that his
statement had been perceived as circumscribing Steven's
creative authority. He'd meant only to emphasize what
Steven had himself told the affiliates following the screening the previous night: "I'm willing to discuss [changing]
anything. I cannot see anything being served by being

arbitrary and close-minded. I'm trying to be sensitive to [your] concerns."

Burke said that he was going to take Steven at his word by telling him he'd found the scenes of lovemaking in the pilot overly long and explicit. Although he was worried about the scale of prospective defections among affiliates, his fundamental objection to these sequences was personal.

Steven acknowledged the crucial importance of the "breakthrough" material in the pilot not playing as gratuitous or ineffective or forced. He said that he would re-examine the lovemaking scenes and consider recutting them in light of Burke's problems with the material. But first Steven needed Dan Burke to recommit to the proposition that, so long as Steven remained within the guidelines he and the network had worked out, the final decision on matters of content would be his.

Burke answered that if Steven undertook a good-faith reconsideration of the lovemaking scenes, he would have Burke's guarantee that—pressure groups, advertiser hesitancy, and affiliate defections notwithstanding—the network would air Steven's version of the pilot as Steven turned it in. He wanted to know if that sounded like a deal. Steven said it did, Burke and Steven shook hands, and Steven flew back to Los Angeles—where we were having actor problems.

* * *

IN ANTICIPATION OF THE company's resuming shooting ten days later, on July 1, we'd made a full distribution of scripts three and four. David Caruso didn't like either one. He felt we'd tilted the storytelling balance in favor of Sipowicz's character, or, as David put it, that we had Kelly wearing a dress.

David and I talked about his concerns. I explained that we had no intention of diminishing David's role or expanding Dennis's. Our goal in these story lines (adapted from the Farley and Gergel cases) was simply to get Sipowicz on his feet, to rehabilitate his character enough that his personal problems would not be a constant, distracting impediment to his and Kelly's effective performance as cops.

I also pointed out to David the various story lines for Kelly in both episodes that were independent of his relationship with Sipowicz. In episode three, Kelly moonlights as a bodyguard for the society wife of a philandering, abusive husband. The woman winds up murdering her husband, and a reluctant Kelly must secure her confession. In the subsequent episode, Kelly's reconciliation with his ex-wife, Laura, is short-circuited when Kelly opposes Laura's working in the District Attorney's Office ("I'm not in the street for you to have to deal with those kind of scumbags"). Laura bristles at what she feels is Kelly's smothering overprotectiveness, which prompts Kelly's own defensive, hurt withdrawal. Kelly also crosses paths again with Laura's infatuated next-door neighbor, Josh Goldstein, who has been so emotionally savaged by a mugging that he's turned ineffectual vigilante. Kelly does his best to counsel and protect "Four B," but can't prevent Goldstein's getting himself shot on a subway car.

It was no sale. David didn't like the material, he wasn't happy, and, as the company came back to work, he wasn't keeping it a secret.

THE BLOWUP CAME DURING a scene between Kelly and Sipowicz in the station-house locker room.

In the action just preceding, Sipowicz, having been rebuffed by Fancy in his request to resume full duties as a detective, has angrily begun rearranging the materials on his desk. ("You know what, fellas? I'm considering a whole new organizational approach on my work area here. See this section, this quadrant I may reserve for those yellow note reminders with the glue on the back. . . . Over here I think I'm gonna restrict to paper weights and animal magnets—maybe those little giraffes.") When the outburst brings Fancy from his office, Sipowicz, sarcastically invoking the enormous workload he's facing, asks to be authorized for overtime. Fancy barely controls his temper. He sets a man-to-man meeting with Sipowicz for that afternoon.

The script now called for Kelly to follow Sipowicz into the locker room, where as one of Sipowicz's responsibilities-in-exile he's looking after fellow detective Greg Medavoy's dog. A frustrated Kelly asks Sipowicz what good he expects to come of having provoked Fancy and having confronted him publicly. In answer, Sipowicz dismisses Fancy's supposed doubts about his readiness to resume active duty, saying they're nothing more than excuses for Fancy's personal and racial dislike for Sipowicz. As much as he wants to work with Kelly again, Sipowicz says that if he has to transfer out of Fancy's command to get back on the street, then that's what he is going to do. And if that's what he has to do, he intends to get his two cents in with Fancy before he goes.

At rehearsal for the locker-room scene, Dennis never got to this climactic final speech. David walked in, shouted, "*What* is the matter with you?" and kicked a metal wastebasket across the floor at Dennis. Then he turned around and walked back out.

Once he got over his surprise, Dennis was furious. It was a child's trick. David didn't like the emotional line of the scene, David hadn't gotten satisfaction in having it changed, so David threw a tantrum. (David would later claim that, rather than displaying temper, he was trying out a piece of business; if this was so, his failure to prepare Dennis only made what he did a different kind of rudeness, and staying in his trailer for fifteen minutes would have played kind of slow on screen.)

What made Dennis more angry was that Greg Hoblit, who later expressed regret for his reaction, left the set without talking to Dennis, wanting to find out what was on David's mind. It was Dennis who had had the wastebasket kicked at him (actually, it had missed his head by only a few feet), Dennis who'd been made to look like a jerk, left with a speech to deliver to a bulldog in an empty room.

Fifteen minutes later, Greg came back from David's trailer and said that David had a point—why was Kelly so endlessly patient with Sipowicz? Now *I* got pissed off. Kelly was *not* the subject of the scene. The story line was geared to be resolved in a subsequent exchange between Sipowicz and *Fancy*. More to the point, if David had a problem, legitimate or not, kicking a wastebasket at Denis's head was not a way he could be allowed to get it on the table.

The blowup and its aftermath established a pattern. David would explode, and a series of destabilizing aftershocks would ensue as people reacted to his conduct; in this case, Dennis wound up pissed off generally, I was pissed off at David and Greg, Greg was pissed off at himself—and David walked back from his trailer, ready to resume shooting.

Over time we tried different ways of dealing with David's behavior on the set. Dennis virtually stopped speaking to him. Jimmy McDaniel took David aside for some private, emphatic dialogue. And there would be conversations of varying tones between Greg and David or David and me or David and Steven or Steven and me and David's manager. These would purchase periods of relative calm, then the bullshit would start all over again.

What was disheartening was to know that all of us, including David, were doing good work, and to be so unsettled and on edge while we were doing it.

Bill celebrates with *Entertainment
Tonight* at his *NYPD Blue* premiere party.

chapter 7

As the time for the premiere approached, both Steven and Dan Burke were standing by their promises: Steven had edited more than fifteen seconds out of the love-making sequences, and ABC, despite continuing pressure from the affiliates, was maintaining its resolve to show *NYPD Blue* as Steven turned it in. Nor was anyone blinking among the show's opponents. The Reverend Donald Wildmon said the American Family Association was receiving tens of thousands of membership signatures from disaffected viewers every day and that preparations for a campaign to boycott *NYPD Blue*'s advertisers were well under way. More than sixty-five ABC stations, including the affiliate in Dallas, the eighth-largest market in the country, either had announced they wouldn't carry the first episode or were still uncommitted to putting it on.

* * *

COPS LIKE TO MARK milestones in their lives: birthdays, marriages, and anniversaries of service—especially retirements. Because their assignments are so various and changing, they're grateful for occasions to reunite with the friends they've made. These get-togethers usually are called "rackets," although more ambitious gatherings tend to get described as "affairs."

Bill had planned a racket for the night the show went on the air. From its humble beginnings—Bill was going to rent the back room of Durow's Bar in Queens and have a six-foot hero sandwich for refreshments—this had grown to a full-scale affair at the Palm Shore Restaurant in Sheepshead Bay; as Bill described it, "a soup-to-nuts prime-rib job with a full Viennese Hour at the finish." The Viennese Hour was a specialty concept of the Palm Shore in which trays of desserts were wheeled from the kitchen and lined up the length of one wall to be eaten by the admiring diners.

Between the daily newspaper accounts about affiliate defections and the difficulties I was reporting on the set, Bill wasn't sure what to do about the party. In addition to contracting the banquet at the Palm Shore, he'd had NYPD balloons made and four hundred T-shirts printed up. "What if they don't put the show on?" Bill asked. "All your other headaches, you'll be pissed off at me for this racket." I told Bill to go ahead (the bills were coming to me). And as I wrote in Los Angeles and he did his daily tours in Queens, we kept working on new stories.

*   *   *

*I DID A GOOD sequence of interviews on a group of cab robberies
that ended with a homicide in the 113th Precinct.*

(This case, with Kelly conducting the interviews of the
tattooed murderer, would form the basis for our eighth
episode, which won the Emmy for best direction.)

*The victim was an off-duty fireman with thirty-two years on his
job, and he was killed the way it happens in most cab robberies, with a bullet in the back of the head. I was working another case—actually the one where I and that detective
Blasie disagreed on who the perp was—when my boss told
me to look at a guy for the cab-driver homicide who'd been
picked up in the One-Thirteen.*

*The guy had been picked out by a driver from one of the
other cab robberies and brought in from his pastor's residence
by Stevie Banks, an RIP [Robbery Intensive Program] detective
from the One-Thirteen, and Maureen Kempton from my
squad. Maureen's son Tim was a professional basketball
player; she was six feet tall herself.*

*Why the guy looked good for the homicide, in one of the
other robberies in the pattern the fare had been picked up at
a location which was the same as the originating point on the
fare where the driver got killed. The driver who'd gotten
robbed off his pickup at this location couldn't describe the*

perp but said he was wearing a maroon type of baseball hat, which the witness driver who had made the ID also said his perp was wearing.

I wanted to sequence the interviews where I'd first take a low-key approach getting the guy to go for the four robberies other than the two with the same originating point. If he went for these, I'd take a more impatient-type tone to move him on the robbery with the same place of origination. If I got him to go for this robbery, then I'd take the gloves off working on him for the homicide.

Of course, nobody said I was from the homicide squad. I was just introduced as Detective Clark from the Borough, with the impression I was some type of supervisor of the detectives already there. And the idea I tried to give, I didn't want to take a lot of time with this interview, I wanted to get things over with.

I told the guy his right approach was packaging the series of four robberies in a single confession, with overall remorse on how he'd been living his life. As opposed to being arrested and rearrested on each robbery and tried separately and looked at as a career criminal, here the judge would react to the incidents under one umbrella. True, a weapon had been used, but there hadn't been violence. With his remorse, he'd be looking at less than five years, and with jail overcrowding, any sentence five years or less, I didn't need to tell him they were looking to put people back on the street.

After a while the guy decided he'd go for the four, and I told him give the nitty-gritty to these other detectives, impressing him that part was essentially mop-up and he was essentially done, and then I left the room.

Fifteen minutes later I came back in, showing this guy I was pretty irritated, where I'd tried to give him a way to go minimizing his exposure relative to jail time, and he paid me back making me a jerk in front of my boss. I told him I was about to leave when my boss asked, "What about this fifth robbery, doesn't this look like the same guy?" and that he'd showed me another file.

At this point I tossed the file in front of the guy on the robbery with the same originating point as the other robbery which wound up a homicide. "My boss is right. This is you. You want to make me look like a fucking jerk, I'll go through the files on every cab robbery in the precinct the last three years and I'll pin every one of 'em on you."

The guy knows he's gotta be careful because of the similarity between the stickup I'm asking him to go for and the one with the shooting in it. On the other hand, if we haven't made the pattern on the originating points and by not cooperating he makes me go and look in the other files and I come up with the other stickup, then he put himself away for twenty more years.

I'd already let him know I wasn't the type guy enjoyed extra legwork. I told him, "You break balls on this, make me go through these other files, say goodbye to your umbrella, you're taking the hit on every one of these cases, every one of 'em gets prosecuted." In other words, if he made me put in overtime, I was returning the favor.

Finally the guy rolled the dice I wasn't already looking at him for the other stickup and he could head me off at the pass. He asked if he went for this fifth one could we put it under the umbrella, and I said all right, but that had better be all of it, and he swore it was. Then we went through the same drill, where I told him give the details to the other detectives and I left the room.

Fifteen minutes later, when I came back into the room again, I told the other detectives to leave. Then I locked the door and I took my watch off and my ring and put them on the table next to me.

I told the guy, "Now we're gonna talk about what I'm here for. I'm a homicide detective, and you murdered a man, an off-duty fireman working a second job to make a few extra dollars to feed his family." I put the file in front of him with the picture of the victim's body. "This fare began the exact same point as the stickup you just went for. This is you. You took this man's life, and you have to understand, if what it takes to make you give that up is laying hands on you, I'm gonna beat you till you beg to die."

After a moment, Bill said, "So, with that, eventually the guy went."

"What does that mean?" I said. " 'Eventually he went'?"

"He went for the homicide."

"I know he went for the homicide. What does 'eventually' mean?"

"Eventually he went," Bill said.

It was the subject that had stopped our conversation when we'd first met. Now Bill and I knew each other better. After another moment he went on.

Understand something. A detective who gets to where he's hypothetically beating on a guy, for all kinds of reasons he's not doing his job. I'm not saying you don't get their attention, but a lot of these guys have stood beatings their whole lives. Your only goal is making the guy understand you're serious with what you're saying, and you're going to accomplish your purpose, and then you go back to his own self-interests.

This case, I immediately asked him, "Now tell me this—I know a lot of these drivers carry weapons. Is it possible this driver had a weapon?" In other words, with having established seriousness, now presenting a best-light scenario for the guy admitting what he did.

After a while he went for that. He said when he'd told the driver to give his money up the driver pulled a gun, and he'd shot him in self-defense. We worked with that. After a few times through the events, I told him he'd never said to me that he'd shit-canned the driver's gun, and if he hadn't shit-canned it and the driver really had a gun we'd've found it at the scene.

"The driver didn't have a gun," I said. "I'm still trying to work with you, and you're still trying to bullshit me"—by my tone there reestablishing seriousness, then going back to self-interest: "Now tell me the truth. Was there a struggle? Did he attempt to grab your weapon?"

Now that's a crucial time for the interview, where you're coming near the truth. The five other robberies had no violence, so my guess was it actually was the driver's trying to protect himself that had moved this guy to kill him, the driver's grabbing for the weapon and so forth. So that's the point in the room the guy may come to feel, if he gives up what actually happened, for the first time since the interview started he won't need to be figuring angles anymore, plus getting to say he isn't a bad guy, he hadn't gone out that night to kill this driver. At that point you'd really want to reestablish in the guy's mind that's the way he should go. You reestablish your seriousness, with getting his attention, and emphasizing he should tell the truth.

"You might hit him then."

Something, again, to bring home your position, your willingness to keep on with this lousy-feeling environment. Raising your voice might be enough.

*   *   *

IN THE END, ALTHOUGH fifty-seven of ABC's 225 affiliates, including Dallas, refused to carry *NYPD Blue*, the premiere received a national rating of 15.4, with a 27 share. (The share tells what percentage of all homes in the country where television is being watched are tuned to that show.) This put us in the top ten among weekly programs. No 10:00 P.M. drama on any of the networks had come close to that ranking in several years.

Our reviews were overwhelmingly favorable, and all the advertising spots were sold out, although Donald Wildmon claimed a moral victory in ABC's having had to cut its rates.

In New York City, our numbers were astronomical, over a 40 share. The New York *Daily News* ran two pages of photos of off-duty uniform cops and detectives watching.

BILL'S PREMIERE PARTY AT the Palm Shore Restaurant went over big. His fellow detectives from Queens Homicide and other detectives he'd worked with through the years and bosses up to the Borough Commander all attended with their wives, and so did Michael Daly and Jimmy Breslin and Dick Schaap. Bill had rented TVs put up all around the Palm Shore's main room, and he called me fifteen or sixteen times while the show was airing in New York. He told me the show was going over great, people were really enjoying it—his dad had even left the dessert area to sit down and watch.

Co-Executive Producer Michael Robin
(*left*) with David on location

chapter 8

I began not to feel well when I was at the racetrack about six weeks after *NYPD Blue*'s premiere.

Gilded Time was running at Santa Anita in the Breeders' Cup Sprint, only his third race in the sixteen months since he'd broken the world record in New Jersey. A month after that race he'd won the $400,000 Arlington Futurity in Chicago, and five weeks after that the $1 million Breeders' Cup Juvenile in Florida, an undefeated campaign which had earned him the Eclipse Award as champion two-year-old in the country.

But in winning his last race, Gilded Time had hurt himself, and he'd endured a further series of leg problems through the whole of the next year. When he finally recovered, his training schedule didn't allow enough time to give him a warm-up race, so we were running him in the national championship for sprinters without one.

Many say this race was the horse's greatest effort. He tracked the leader to the head of the stretch, then began closing on the outside. With an eighth of a mile to go, Gilded Time had almost drawn even, but his lack of conditioning finally told. As the racetrack expression has it, the horse "got late." Even so, he was beaten less than a length for all the money.

During the stretch run I began to feel pressure in my chest, and like I might get sick to my stomach. I tried to pass this off as the moment's excitement, although I'd had exciting moments at the track without these accompanying sensations.

THE FOLLOWING MONDAY I went with the company to New York for ten days of shooting. It was our third time in the city, but the first since we'd gone on the air. People shouted greetings to the actors from passing cars and street corners and gave advice about story lines and relationships. Sherry Stringfield was repeatedly urged to reconcile with Kelly and Amy Brenneman to leave him alone. Nicky Turturro, who had a number of street scenes to do with Luis Guzman, the superb New York actor who plays his father, turned out to have a large and vocal number of female teenage fans.

Although David and Dennis were getting star treatment in the media (in a cover story, *TV Guide* had already tagged David "The Sex Symbol of the New Season"; Dennis was on its cover later in the year as "The Cop You Hate to Love"), people in New York seemed to react to them less as celebrities than with affectionate familiarity. Cops took to Dennis especially. Greg Hoblit, who'd been part of the success of both *Hill Street* and *L.A. Law*, turned to me one morning as we watched passersby respond to David and Dennis and said, "This is when you know your show's a hit."

It was true. Our national audience share had stabilized in the mid-twenties. It was four or five points higher in the thirty largest markets, and in the high thirties in New York. A small number of the stations who'd initially refused to carry *NYPD Blue* had reconsidered, and in other "dark" markets ABC was allowing competing independent stations to purchase the show and air it. In Dallas on Tuesday nights, bars that could get *NYPD Blue* on their satellite dishes were doing big business.

ON THIS TRIP WE were shooting scenes from five different episodes (eight through twelve), which would air in early winter. The logistical problems caused by working simultaneously from so many different scripts in such a short time are enormous, but it was the only way the trips to the city were economically feasible.

The scripts banked during the long delay in getting *NYPD Blue* on the air had now been used up. The scripts for these winter shows weren't finished yet, and I was working pretty hard on the set getting scenes written and rewritten.

The biggest headache was a scene from show twelve, set outside the precinct station house, whose purpose was to salvage for use a rooftop sequence already shot for show seven on an earlier trip but cut because of that episode's length. Steven said he wasn't going to let go of a $40,000 sequence without a fight, so we'd structured the story materials of the twelfth episode to try to make the roof-top footage fit.

The setup scene had to make credible the exits from the station house of Kelly and Laura, then of Tom Towles, playing the head of the Organized Crime Unit, then of Fancy and the OCC boss's chauffeur, all of whom except for Laura then drive away from the station house in separate cars in an order and at intervals that would square with the footage we already had showing the staggered time of their arrival on the rooftop where a button man for the mob, the assassin of Alfonse Giardella, has been cornered and is holding a hostage.

It wasn't Shakespeare, but we more or less got the scene to work. I even wrote in a scene earlier in the episode showing a wino who's been collared for exposing himself in honor of the surprisingly warm January weather (the original footage had been shot in July).

ON OUR FINAL DAY of shooting, the production call was for five-thirty in the morning; daylight is precious in mid-November, and we had to get our first shot at sunrise. We were in Harlem, on 135th Street near the Hudson River. The scene we were to shoot showed the arrest of the tattooed man Luis, whom Kelly would interrogate and eventually get to confess in the cab-driver homicide. It was cold and the wind was blowing off the water. I remember thinking as the sun came up how beautiful the city looked in the first light, and that I was getting old—I'd never felt so tired.

A FEW DAYS LATER I was called to the set during rehearsals for the sequence in our twelfth episode in which Kelly makes it possible for Licalsi to destroy evidence connecting her to Angelo Marino, the mob boss who has been blackmailing her, and whom Kelly suspects she has murdered.

Kelly has told Licalsi the journal that contains her name is lying on his desk in the empty squad room. As Licalsi enters the squad room, Kelly remains in the hallway, choosing to stand at an angle that prevents his seeing what Licalsi does. Kelly now notes Martinez descending the stairs from the upper floor. The younger cop pauses to express gratitude to Kelly for the help he's given him in learning interrogation techniques, and, with a more general, awkward sincerity, for teaching him to be the kind of cop Kelly is.

The sequence is crosshatched with ironies, and Michael Robin, our supervising producer, who was directing the episode, was having difficulties with David about its staging.

In fact, these difficulties were part of David's discovering what tonalities in the scene he wanted to play; part of his process at this preliminary stage is to fulminate and argue. But in this instance, in front of the full production unit that had gathered for rehearsal, he'd shouted there was no way to make shit like this work, then, demeaning Michael, insisted on talking about changes with someone senior to him in authority.

It was my turn in the barrel. David and I went to one side of the station-house set. We talked out the alternative implications of Kelly's situating himself on the stairs in a way that prevented Martinez's entering the squad room, or of his standing to one side, allowing Martinez to converse with him as long as Martinez wished, but making no active effort to distract him or delay his moving past. It was the difference between portraying Kelly as an active intercessor in protecting Licalsi or a more neutral witness to the situation's outcome.

As was almost always the case, David had his finger on an important ambiguity. And, also as always, his behavior had created a series of separate difficulties: the company was stalled; Michael was furious at having been publicly embarrassed; I resented being made an accomplice to Michael's embarrassment because of the need to get rehearsal resumed, not to mention having had to walk away from writing an episode (the thirteenth) already in its third day of preproduction without our yet having published the script. The bonus was getting to respond respectfully to someone who'd just described my work as shit.

As David and I talked, the pressure in my chest returned and extended into my left arm. I felt nauseated and began to sweat. I sat down on the floor. David and I finally decided his performance in the scene would walk the line between the two interpretations, leaving it to the viewer to decide whether Kelly would have tried to stop Martinez if he had attempted to enter the squad room. Then I walked off the set and called my doctor.

AN ELECTROCARDIOGRAM WAS NORMAL, but my doctor explained that these often aren't definitively diagnostic. He set up a thalium stress test, in which dye is injected into the vein while the patient's heart rate is elevated by ex-

ercise, then a series of X-ray pictures is taken, followed
by another series twenty-four hours later. The X-rays indicate how much blood is getting to the various areas of
the heart.

Bill was staying with us in Los Angeles. He'd flown in
to help Greg Hoblit prepare the staging of a particularly
complicated street scene in episode thirteen in which a
newly transferred female detective (played by Wendy Mc-
Kenna) sees her husband (also a detective) murdered as
he tries to prevent a robbery.

That night, at home, I told Bill I hadn't been feeling
well and was going to have medical tests the following day.
I didn't want to drive alone, because I was still experi-
encing chest symptoms, but since I wasn't sure the symptoms were heart-related I didn't want to worry Rita by
telling her how I felt.

Bill drove me to the hospital early the following morning—for reasons too complicated to explain, this was in
Pasadena, a forty-minute drive away. We got the first half
of the test done, then went to work, and went back the
next morning so the comparison set of photos could be
taken.

Both mornings, Bill sat with me in the nuclear-imaging
room of the hospital basement. Lying facedown and im-
mobile for the forty-five-minute sessions of X-ray photog-
raphy, I had to listen to Bill endlessly rehearsing his lines

from a scene in *L.A. Law,* whose executive producer, Billy Finklestein, had asked Bill to play the role of a detective giving a deposition. I can best evoke Bill's performance by comparing it to the scene in the first *Godfather* film in which, as Vito Corleone receives his wedding guests in a nearby office, Luca Brazzi sits miserably in the courtyard, rehearsing the three sentences of congratulation he will pronounce to the Godfather on the occasion of his daughter's wedding.

That second afternoon, the doctor called the studio with my test results: the pictures showed that two areas of my heart weren't getting enough blood. Given my symptoms, he thought I might need immediate treatment and should come back to the hospital.

I got a ride home (Bill had gone to the *L.A. Law* soundstage to shoot his scene), and talked to Rita. We spoke to the children, then drove to the hospital in fits and starts through the rush-hour traffic.

Bill found out what was happening when, halfway through his scene, my assistant came to the set to say that with my being hospitalized she'd arranged for him to have a rental car. Bill couldn't remember his speeches anymore. They wrote them out for him on cue cards, which were placed around the set out of camera view. Bill did his lines once, then drove to Pasadena.

* * *

THE DOCTORS PERFORMED AN angiogram the next morning, threading a catheter into my heart through an artery in my thigh. This allowed them to get an even more specific picture of what was going on.

I turned out to have a left-dominant heart, meaning a major part of the blood flow moves through what's called the circumflex artery. The angiogram showed that this artery was more than 90 percent closed, and that another less important artery was about 70 percent blocked. I was marginally conscious through the procedure (patients who want to can watch on a TV screen as the catheter moves through their arteries, but I turned this opportunity down). I do remember the doctor saying, when he'd moved the catheter into the circumflex artery, that the artery had a "significant lesion," and that they would need to do an angioplasty to restore the flow of blood. This procedure involves threading a deflated balloon through the hollow catheter, then inflating the balloon when it gets to where the artery is narrowed. The inflated balloon forces the artery walls back open and restores a channel for blood to get through.

When the balloon was inflated, my chest hurt about the way it had at the racetrack and on the set. The doctor explained this was because the balloon was completely cutting off blood flow. He said that when the balloon was deflated the pain would go away and the artery should remain open. (The procedure has around a 35 percent rate of failure; if the artery is going to close down again, or restenose, it tends to happen within the first year.)

The balloon was deflated, and the pain did subside. Then the doctor worked for a while on the other blockage, but because the narrowed portion of that artery was near a junction with yet another arterial wall, he was afraid too much manipulation of the catheter might cause a tear. He said he felt this artery had adequate blood flow and we should quit while we were ahead. I told the doctor I was with him.

Sipowitz and disgraced cop Roberts
(Michael Harney) preparing for a scene
Used by permission of Capital Cities/
ABC, Inc.

chapter 9

The next morning the doctors saw what they called "subtle" changes in my heartbeat and thought that one of the arteries they'd worked on might be closing down. They still had a tube in my thigh and decided to do another angiogram.

The catheterization showed the circumflex artery was open enough, so the doctor tried again to widen the passage in the other occluded artery, but he still couldn't do it. Later in the day, he told me that if this blockage did cause a heart attack, the area affected probably wouldn't be so large as to prevent my living a normal life.

That was part of a conversation we had about my prospects and what changes I might consider in lifestyle. The blockages were caused by coronary artery disease. The doctor explained that the course of the disease could be affected by diet, weight, exercise, and stress.

I'd already given up some bad habits, although I still had a big pool available. I was ready to make adjustments. What I hoped I wouldn't have to do was give up working on the show.

For me, the regimen of deadlines and responsibilities imposed by a television series had been a type of liberation. I had no great wistfulness about periods in my life that had been less encumbered but tended to end in unfamiliar cities and rooms.

In urging me to cut back on my professional obligations, my doctor had suggested my primary goal should be to live to watch my children grow up. However provisionally, I understood myself well enough to know that my best chance at this outcome was to have a demanding and ordered routine, and to do work I was proud of.

I was proud of *NYPD Blue.* I also knew a unique combination of circumstances had put us in a position to take advantage of our excellence, and that was a rare chance.

UNTIL NOW, AS THE writing producer, once I'd talked with Steven and Bill about the stories in a given episode and we'd outlined its scenes, I'd been in charge of each script's further development. If I wasn't the primary writer, I supervised our staff or free-lance authors while the script was being written, polished the final draft, then worked through the preproduction process with the heads of the other production areas—the casting person, set designer, location scout, and director—making whatever script adjustments were needed.

Although Steven had a company to run, including getting another new series (*The Byrds of Paradise*) on its feet, after my hospitalization he took on the writing producer's liaison responsibilities. But he didn't have the time or inclination to do the writing itself, and the show was still too early in its development to be staff-written without the seams showing. Steven and I agreed that if my health held up my job would still be getting the scripts out, but now with an emotional equanimity worthy of my new hero, Deepak Chopra.

AFTER I GOT OUT of the hospital, Bill would work his full weekly chart as a detective, then fly back and forth across the country to spend his two days off at our house. He went with me on walks as I built up my tolerance for exercise. He even started on the nonfat diet I'd been prescribed, although he quit that after a day.

His tone about my health problems was casual and positive. He said when they put him in the ground, I'd be at the ceremony, tossing carnations. When we were in the hospital in Pasadena he'd keep up a running banter with the nurses and technicians. Once, when I had to be readmitted, he confided quietly to a lab assistant who was taking my blood pressure: "He seemed to be doing better, then he started to overdo, training for these Gay Olympics."

Sometimes Bill's deeper feelings would show through. Several days later, when the doctors had decided to do yet another angiogram, Bill said to Rita, "I know David's going to be all right, because God wouldn't take my brother away and him too."

"HERE'S A STORY," BILL said on one of our walks. "I know there's something in it, but we help a wrong cop."

I wasn't sure I followed that, but asked what the story was.

On the four-to-twelve the body of a twenty-six-year-old girl showed up floating in a little creek in the 106th Precinct. This girl was known to the 106th Squad previously from having notified them she'd seen her boyfriend bury a body in the backyard of his house. The body turned out was the business partner of the boyfriend, and the boyfriend got collared.

This girl was a drug user, a heroin addict. After her boyfriend went to jail she'd become an informant for the 106th Squad and got involved with one of the detectives, to the point he got her an apartment and furniture and paid the phone bills. Then, apparently, being a drug user, and not having the type relationship she wanted with this married cop, she'd ended up severing ties with him, and then took her own life.

The relationship was pretty much common knowledge in the squad, so the detective who caught the case called his boss at home that night concerning how to handle that aspect. The boss had a first-grade detective in the squad who he figured both knew the dead girl as a stoolie and, since it was a suicide with no charges to pursue, would also know how to try to keep the detective out of it who'd been involved with her, protecting the guy's family and so forth. The first-grade detective went to the girl's house and, unbelievably, while the building superintendent was standing there, removed some photographs of the detective and the girl from their picture frames and walked out of the apartment with them.

What else happened, later in the day a cab driver came into the squad with some of the dead girl's things—apparently on her way to drown herself she had gone to her mother's house in a cab, then when the mother wasn't home she gave the cabbie a few dollars extra and asked him to drop the stuff off with her mother the next day—but when the cabbie heard the girl was dead he brought the items to the squad.

One of the items was a diary which basically read as a suicide note, and also had the detective's name in it who had the re-

*lationship with this girl. Instead of vouchering it, the first-grade
detective who was running the case put the diary in his locker.*

*At the funeral, the detective with the personal relationship
with the dead girl, a married man, stands at the coffin crying.
The girl's mother knew nothing about her daughter being a
junkie or her relationship with the detective. No parent wants
to believe their child committed suicide, so when the mother
finds out about this detective having the secret relationship
with her daughter, she started asking questions, had he
maybe been involved with her dying, was there foul play, going
to the press and so forth.*

*Once the story got in the press, field investigators from IAB
got involved. They wound up finding the diary the first-grade
detective had forgot he even had in his locker. There was no
question of this being a suicide, but by the time IAB was done,
the lieutenant, who was a good man, had to leave the department—he only avoided charges because they hadn't gotten
filed within the thirty-day limit—and the first-grade detective
had to retire too, and the original catching detective also took
a hit.*

*The detective who was involved with the girl, who was really
the only bad guy in the story, also left the department, on
"best interest," which is a reduced pension, then he wound up
blowing his next job on some nickel-and-dime scam on his ex-
pense vouchers. He'd already blown his marriage telling his
wife they couldn't afford things and then her finding out in the*

*papers he'd bought this other girl a sofa and paid her rent
and phone bill.*

After a minute Bill looked at me. "See, I know we could
do something with that, but we wouldn't have space in the
one script to bring both this wrong detective in and some
other new guys who tried to help him, but I know we
wouldn't want to make *our* guys look bad, reaching out to
help this type of guy themselves."

I realized Bill was trying to think not as a cop but as a
storyteller, trying to help me out.

WE USED THIS STORY in episode fifteen, addressing the
dramatic problem Bill had identified by having "our guys"
make less of an effort to protect Roberts, the bad cop, who
was wonderfully played by Michael Harney.

This was the first episode we did after I came out of the
hospital, and I made a conscious effort to stand back while
it was being written. The author was a free-lance writer
name Ann Biderman, and the script won the Emmy.

Sipowitz introduces Miss Abandondo
(Gail O'Grady) to Medavoy (Gordon
Clapp). *Used by permission of Capital
Cities/ABC, Inc.*

chapter 10

The award season begins in late January. The first of these is the Golden Globes, given by the Hollywood Foreign Press Association, which named *NYPD Blue* best drama and David best dramatic actor. David gave a generous acceptance speech at the award banquet, saying he shared his honor with Dennis, who hadn't won in a catch-all supporting-actor category which included variety shows and comedies.

Later in the spring, the People's Choice Awards selected *NYPD Blue* most popular new show and most popular drama series overall. We also won the Humanitas Prize for best writing (this was the cash prize which ten years before had started me on the bumpy road of horse ownership), and the Producers Guild named Steven, Greg, and me producers of the year.

I'd been around enough to have some perspective on winning and not winning awards, but it was gratifying to see critical attention shift to the quality of the show and our actors' performances instead of the quota of dirty words in a given episode or the muscle tone of David's butt.

AS THE SEASON MOVED toward its end, Steven and I considered which characters and relationships should receive primary focus in our concluding story lines.

Among the additions to the cast after our first two episodes, Gordon Clapp as Gregory Medavoy and Gail O'Grady as Donna Abandondo had taken hold most successfully. When we'd introduced Gordon's character, all we knew about him was that he had a pet named Luther (in the third episode, while Sipowicz is on suspension from street duty, it's Medavoy who asks him to feed and walk his bulldog). At his audition for the role, Gordon played Medavoy with a shy, stammering hesitancy which showed us the character's possibilities as a foil for Sipowicz's blustery impatience. Gordon was cast, and Medavoy became a fixture in the squad.

The character of Donna Abandondo, the well-built civilian aide, had been proposed by Bill. Originally we'd planned to keep her personal life a mystery, making Donna an object of gossip and speculation among the precinct detectives. But Gail O'Grady had added to the character's sexual appeal a self-possession and decency which made Donna a more interesting subject for storytelling. The result was her romantic involvement with the soon-to-be-divorced Medavoy, an arc we saw extending well into the second season.

We weren't so satisfied with the development of the women in Kelly's life. Through the season's first half, we'd worked to situate Laura, Sherry Stringfield's character, as a "riding DA"—a member of the District Attorney's Office who covers cases in a number of precincts in the borough, including Kelly's. We wanted Laura to have consistent access to the 15th Squad because our stories focused on the workplace—if Laura and Kelly didn't get to spend time with each other professionally, their relationship inevitably would lose narrative importance.

Our problem was that an attraction we *hadn't* planned on had developed between Sipowicz and Sharon Lawrence's character, Sylvia Costas, who was also a riding DA. The uncertain courtship between Sipowicz and Costas engagingly dramatized Sipowicz's effort to make his way emotionally in his recovery from alcoholism. The result was that story lines involving a detective coming into contact with a riding DA—the natural occasion for scenes between David and Sherry—instead were going to Dennis and Sharon. In effect, Laura became a casualty of the Sipowicz/Costas relationship.

While we were considering ways to keep Sherry's character in play—we'd just introduced a second romantic interest for Laura, an upscale midtown doctor who takes a genially patronizing attitude toward Kelly—Sherry asked for a meeting with Steven and me.

With the good spirit she'd shown throughout the season, Sherry said she recognized that we were having problems writing for Laura. She asked if we'd consider releasing her from her contract. Steven and I both felt guilty about not having done a better job serving the character, but we agreed to Sherry's request. Leaving *NYPD Blue* was a great decision for Sherry, who the next season became one of the leads on *ER*, the highest-rated show on television.

We'd had storytelling problems of a different sort with Janice Licalsi, Kelly's other original romantic interest.

Licalsi's assassination of Angelo Marino, the mob boss who'd been blackmailing her, and Kelly's decision, once he'd identified Licalsi's involvement, to help her escape detection, had allowed us to explore at a number of levels the differences between a cop's sense of right and wrong and the legal standards of justice. But Steven and I always had felt that after getting away with Marino's murder, in some fashion Licalsi would pass judgment on herself for what she'd done. Similarly, we believed that while Kelly would not feel obligated to expose Licalsi to the judgments of a legal system whose inequities he experienced every day, once he'd protected her, his personal values wouldn't permit him to sustain their relationship.

We played out these story turns through the middle episodes of the season, concluding with Licalsi's preemptive decision, after Kelly has made it possible for her to destroy the evidence which would have incriminated her, that she and Kelly should stop seeing each other. "Maybe not right away, Johnny," Licalsi tells Kelly, "but someday if we stayed together I'd look at you and see you hating me 'cause of what you did for me."

Like the characters themselves, with Kelly and Licalsi separated, Steven and I now came up against the difficulty of getting past Licalsi's crime. That is, while we felt the possibilities of the arc had been played out, we couldn't formulate credible story lines for Amy Brenneman's character which moved beyond her struggle to live with her guilt, or the ironies of her not having been caught.

We talked with Amy, who agreed with our assessment of the storytelling box we'd put her character in. We decided that in the season's final story sequence, over Kelly's objections, Licalsi would confess and be arrested.

THE MOST FRUSTRATING CASE in Bill's career involved the abduction of a twelve-year-old girl, Antonella Mattina. Bill believed he knew the perpetrator's identity, but he couldn't make an arrest.

On a day tour one afternoon around three o'clock, I got a call, a mother said her daughter had gone to the bank to make a deposit at eleven-thirty that morning and she hadn't come back home.

I went to the residence and Phil Auerbach was there. The mother was an Italian woman who was very distraught. Her sister and brother were there with her.

The mother said she'd given her daughter eight thousand dollars in checks to deposit at the CitiBank branch five blocks from the house. The daughter, Antonella, had made the deposit, and afterward she was on the bank's camera going out the front door. After that no one saw her.

The father came home. He was distraught also, from an understandable reaction but also feeling guilty because of his being the one who'd started letting Antonella make bank deposits. It had made the father proud how everyone in the neighborhood knew this was his daughter and he was such a success story and well liked—he was a big painting contractor—that she could be safe carrying money on the street.

I had Aviation check the rooftops and Harbor check the water, even though we were a good fifteen blocks away, and also Auxiliary Forces came in and we did a door-to-door in a wide area including a large housing development near there.

Also every available canine unit came in. We searched through the night and all the following morning, but nothing came up.

As early as that first night the father, in trying to just do anything he could to find his daughter, reached out to several private investigators. All these guys did was call our squad to see if we had anything, then they took this man's money. They saw fit to do this to the father in his terror and need. Later on, one after another, a lineup of psychics did the same thing.

That first night we set up a trap on the Mattinas' phone and trapped a call that came back to 146-15 22nd Avenue. We went to this house and three people were there, Deidre Crowley, who was a thirteen-year-old teenager, Patrick Crowley, Jr., who was nineteen, and the father, Patrick Crowley, Sr. Deidre, the teenage girl, was a friend of Antonella's. They all said they hadn't made the phone call to the Mattinas' house.

The girl, Deidre, was credible in her manner and upset with finding out Antonella was missing and wouldn't have had a reason to deny making the call. I put my follow-up questions to the males. The father seemed very feminine. The nineteen-year-old son was just strange, not meeting my eyes and a mumbly type. After a while we left.

The next morning we checked with telephone security and confirmed the call had in fact come from the Crowley house. I went back there with Sergeant Gene Albright and Tony Lombardi from Missing Persons who worked the case the whole time. When we rang the bell a middle-aged woman looked out the upstairs window and said she'd be right down. We waited ten minutes, then this woman opened up wearing only a T-shirt and panties. So here was a feminine father, an exhibitionist mother, and a weird-type son who would've had access to the missing girl through his sister's friendship with Antonella. I wanted to look at the father somewhat but especially at the son for maybe having been involved.

We asked this woman parading around in her panties to reach out to her son where he worked, and was it all right meanwhile for us to look around. We put the request on a sympathy basis, where both Mattina parents were having visions of their daughter trapped somewhere in a closet—they were both having visions, which got worse as time went on—and told this woman that to calm the parents from being so distraught we were looking in the closets at all the houses we stopped at. The woman said go ahead, so this was how we got to look in her son's room.

As we were doing this, the woman screamed into the telephone where she'd called her son at work, "Don't you talk to me that way." The son had got very upset with his mother allowing the search. I said to the mother, well, we'd like to talk to him, and she said we should leave his room and when he came home she'd call us.

When we left the house we went straight to the apartment building where this kid worked in maintenance and they told us he'd taken off for the day. We spoke to his supervisor and he told me the previous day Crowley had said to him the police might be there asking questions. The super said part of Crowley's job was to dispose of the trash.

We called Emergency Services and had them search the building incinerator. They collected pails and pails of ashes, but going through them they didn't come up with anything.

Meanwhile I called the Crowleys back, asking where their son was, but at this point the father said he'd hired an attorney for Patrick Jr. and the attorney had instructed him not to let his son talk to me. I said, I don't understand, we're looking for a missing kid, if Crowley Sr. didn't allow me to interview his son he was making him a suspect. The father said he had spoken to legal counsel and this was what he was advised.

This kid had no record, but everyone I talked to said he was a twitch. At his senior prom, he'd taken a thirteen-year-old girl for his date. Even with liking him as a suspect, with his being lawyered up and no other evidence coming in we had no way to go on him.

I worked the case for months, and it went nowhere. The pressure bore down worse on Antonella's parents with them getting visions of where she might be and psychics and private investigators feeding on them. Once, CNN showed a ship trapped on a sandbar in the Gulf of Mexico and the father was convinced his daughter was trapped in the ship. I had to keep him from flying down. Even after they took the Chinese people off who'd been hidden inside and were trying to sneak *into America, Mr. Mattina kept having a vision of Antonella trapped below the deck of this ship in a closet where the door hadn't been opened when the Coast Guard was going through it.*

Besides the PIs and psychics running games on this family, people tried to extort them. The parents would get calls or letters saying Antonella was buried underground in this place or that with a few days of food and water left. I'd have to talk the father out of leaving the money while we checked out these bogus calls. He wanted to leave the money, so he could believe he'd get his daughter back.

Plus, warpos would reach out to these people. One guy called saying the mother had to stand in the doorway of her house at a certain time each day for three days in a row rubbing her private parts, and on the third day if she'd rubbed herself consecutively and they left a certain amount of money under a mailbox, he'd let the daughter go.

Four years later the New York State Police collared two guys poaching deer, and bringing them out of the woods they came across a young person's skull with braces on the teeth, which Antonella had had.

I went upstate with Tony Lombardi and some Emergency Service cops and after we searched two hours we found an arm fifty-five feet away from where the skull was discovered, then the skeleton of the torso ten feet from there, with remains of the clothes Antonella had been wearing when she disap-

peared. Plants had grown up and down through the body for four years, so all the cotton on the cotton-polyester blouse was gone, but the polyester was still left.

We'd worked hard on that case. At the end, with discovering Antonella's bones, all we could think to do was dig far down in the ground to lift the earth up without disturbing her remains. Afterward, everyone got sick off the poison oak growing all over that area.

It turned out Patrick Crowley, Jr., had a relative living upstate only a few miles from where we found Antonella's body. I knew it was probably a loser, but we got the DA to take what we had on Patrick Crowley, Jr., to the Grand Jury. The Grand Jury didn't indict him.

Every year, Crowley got Christmas cards signed Antonella Mattina, and he got them on her birthdays too. On holidays like July the Fourth, if he was having a barbecue outside, I'd sometimes stand on the street across from his house. I wanted him to see me, to know someone remembered this was another holiday Antonella Mattina hadn't got to be with her family.

Even so, I felt like I'd let that family down.

WE DID A STORY suggested by the Mattina case in our seventeenth episode. Sipowicz thwarts a private investigator who's working in concert with a psychic to fleece a grieving father. (The father, Dominic Bucci, is played by the extraordinary character actor Louis Giambalvo, who'd portrayed the brother-in-law of ne'er-do-well Detective J. D. Larue on *Hill Street*.) The emotional focus of the story is Sipowicz's support of a man who, after two years, still cannot accept the likelihood that his daughter is dead.

My beloved college professor Robert Penn Warren taught me that the secret subject of any story worth telling is what we learn or fail to learn over time. It's a particular challenge to structure stories in television drama to illuminate rather than distort this theme.

We set the Dominic Bucci story two years after his daughter's disappearance to establish that it's not the first shock of his loss which has prevented Mr. Bucci from closing with what has happened, but rather the father's harrowing sense of personal guilt which effectively has frozen him in the past, at the moment of his daughter's disappearance. Time's passage too exposes Sipowicz's strength of spirit as he keeps watch with Mr. Bucci, doing what he can to make the truth available to him while respecting the father's right to accept or reject it.

As with the father of Antonella Mattina, when cases he works involve the murder of a child, Bill makes a particular effort to keep contact with the victim's parents. On

Bill with old friends Jimmy Breslin and Dick Schaap

VERY PLACE IS SAFE TO HIM WHO LIV

David and Bill
before David lost fifty
pounds

GILDED TIME:
TOPS AMONG
2-YEAR-OLDS

David's Thoroughbred,
who won the Breeders'
Cup Juvenile

Paddy Nugent—Bill's former
partner who used to dunk his
upper bridge in strangers' drinks

Bill's friend Detective Sergeant Karen Krizan makes the cover of *New York* magazine.

Sipowitz interrogating a "perp"

Martinez (Nicholas Turturro)
preparing for a scene with his father
(Luis Guzman)

Fireman/cab driver's killer gets
busted on *NYPD Blue*.

11   ▷ 11A   12   ▷ 12A   13   ▷ 13A

In the first season
finale, Licalsi
(Amy Brennerman) is
arrested for
killing Marino and
his driver.

The second
season
begins with
Licalsi's trial
for double
murder.

Publicity still introducing Bobby Simone (Jimmy Smits)

The *Daily News* took note when Bill spent time in New York showing Jimmy the ropes.

MY STUDENT SMITS

Sipowitz goes undercover in the show's third season.

Sipowitz and
Costas
share domestic
bliss.

holidays he spends hours roasting up turkeys with all the fixings, and, along with his friends, he includes such parents on his delivery list.

One of these is Ronald Shalit, an Israeli man whose son David was murdered while working alone in the trailer of his father's used-car lot. Bill caught David Shalit's killers—I've watched the videotaped confession of one of them as he describes the fifteen-year-old boy asking not to be killed while the murderer was probing with his gun inside the bag he'd used to cover the boy's head until, finding the point between David Shalit's eyes, he pulled the trigger.

After his son's death, Ronald Shalit withdrew from the world. He sold his used-car lot and almost never left his house except to pray daily at temple for his son's soul. Bill was one of the few people with whom Shalit stayed in contact.

While Bill was in California, Mr. Shalit had occasion to return Bill's acts of friendship. Bill was buying his daughter Natalie a used car, and in her father's absence, Mr. Shalit offered to accompany Natalie to a used-car auction in Rockland County to make sure she wasn't sold a lemon.

Bill's mention of Mr. Shalit's helping Natalie and how he'd come to know him made me think about revisiting the Bucci story. We'd come to the end of the first season.

I felt we'd proved the tenacity and goodness of our cops' natures, and that if it was these qualities of character, tested by time, which put Sipowicz in position to get lucky, it would not be unjustifiably sentimental to show him happening into the Bucci case's solution. In tribute to Mr. Shalit, I put Sipowicz at a used-car auction, where Sipowicz has gone with his son and Mr. Bucci to find a car for Andy Jr. when he discovers the Bucci child's abductor.

Steven then suggested that not only should the girl's abductor be caught, but Mr. Bucci's daughter should be discovered alive.

ONCE, AN INTERVIEWER REMARKED to Henry James that the character of Fleda Vetch, the heroine of his novel *The Spoils of Poynton*, was so virtuous that the interviewer doubted events such as she initiated would occur in real life. James replied, "So much the worse for Real Life."

Bill and Bobby Simone (Jimmy Smits)
*Used by permission of Capital Cities/ABC,
Inc.*

chapter 11

When shooting finished for the 1993–1994 season, we flew to New York so I could spend time with friends of Bill's. He introduced me to Tommy Doyle, who is sixty-five and white-haired and at five feet eight inches weighs no more than 150 pounds, but who Bill guaranteed was the toughest guy he'd ever seen on a beat.

Tommy could have gotten his gold shield years before, but he'd wanted to keep working on the street. Finally, he was offered a position as a detective who would train other street cops. Tommy would accept only if, even though he'd be promoted out of uniform, he could remain a delegate of the Policemen's Benevolent Association. The union made the exception, and Tommy took his shield.

Tommy told me it was simple to be a cop, that you only had to know four things—people, places, the things they did, and the times they did them. If you knew that about your beat you knew everything. I also met Tommy's younger brother, who told me that when he had joined the force, Tommy had said to him, "This is a good job for us. We've got no education but we can read and write and we're honest people. Don't ever embarrass this Job."

Also on this trip, on a warm spring day in the 72nd Precinct in Brooklyn, Bill and I encountered a thirty-five-year-old man walking the streets wearing a parka who, hailing Bill, delivered a wandering monologue. The super of his building had taken some of his possessions and refused to return them. Bill said he'd have the situation looked into—in fact, he told the young man he'd have Tommy Doyle look into it; the 72nd was Tommy's precinct.

After we'd walked away, Bill explained this was the son of Henny Ryan, whom Bill had known for twenty-five years, since just after he'd come on The Job. At that point Bill spent his spare time hanging around a pet store that Henny also frequented. They were both pigeon fliers. Henny also was what is known as a mungo guy, someone who dealt in stolen infrastructure—pipe and other materials from construction sites—but, as Bill explained, Henny was a nice guy, and because of their mutual interest in birds, they became and remained friends. Bill would sometimes go with Henny on the visits Henny made every weekend to sit on the sand at Coney Island Beach, where he hadn't been allowed to swim when he was a child and partially crippled by polio.

Now Henny was senile and in a nursing home, and as a favor to Bill, the cops in the 72nd Precinct would do what they could to keep an eye on Henny's son, who was well-intentioned but unstable and prone to violence. Later, when Bill talked to Tommy Doyle about the boy's alleged problem with his super, Tommy said he'd tried three times to look into it, but the boy's claims didn't seem to have any basis. Tommy and Bill both felt bad for Henny's son, but he refused medical treatment, and they didn't know how else to get him help.

In our second season, I based my characterization of the emotionally disturbed son of Sipowicz's AA sponsor, who eventually kills his father, on my impressions of this sad young man.

AS WE BEGAN PREPARING the scripts for the new season, I developed more heart problems. The doctors determined one of my arteries had closed back down and did another balloon procedure trying to reopen it. But I still felt lousy afterward, and on a trip to Buffalo to visit family was put back into the hospital, where the doctors did another angiogram and found a problem with a different artery. They said I should be taken to the Cleveland Clinic, where a new procedure to open arteries was being done with a type of drill instead of balloons.

While Bill, for reasons that still elude me, memorialized the occasion with his Kodak, I was put on an air ambulance and flown to the Cleveland Clinic. My heart went out of its proper rhythm as the procedure was being performed, beating too strongly and quickly like it was about to blow out of my chest, but the doctors were able to get it reregulated (of my getting past this difficulty during the operation, my brother Bob, a surgeon who'd flown on the air ambulance to Cleveland, later remarked quietly, "Sometimes it's nice to steal one"). The doctors felt that the drilling itself had been successful and were hopeful the artery would now stay open.

I've had better between-season vacations, and have Bill's pictures to prove it.

IN OUR BUSINESS, FOR the lead actor in the second year of a successful series to try to better his deal is the rule rather than the exception. So I wasn't surprised, on my return to Los Angeles, when Steven told me David Caruso's representatives wanted to renegotiate his contract. But Steven said the demands David's representatives were making were nuts.

They'd asked for a raise that in itself would put the show wildly over budget, as well as causing a reverberating effect on other salaries; they'd itemized a list of perks David would require if he returned, which ran the gamut from the more or less standard upgrade to a bigger trailer to our paying the salary of a film-development person for David and up to his right to opt out of a third of our episodes if a film opportunity presented itself. David also wanted us to redress what he felt had been a punitive reduction of Kelly's role in favor of Sipowicz's during the last half of the previous season. How to do this with David missing in up to a third of the shows would be up to us.

As had been the case when he was negotiating with ABC, Steven kept me on the sidelines while he talked with David's agents and lawyers and manager—my problem, at moments requiring diplomacy, is that I lack impulse control. But at the end of each day he'd give me a war report, and these indicated his growing reluctance to accede to the Caruso camp's demands.

Steven finally counterproposed a renewal of David's contract with an increase beyond what had previously been negotiated, with further incentive payments based on David's not causing us to lose time during shooting. The amount of the incentive payment would be computed according to reductions in what was called "The Caruso Hour"—the estimated amount of additional time it took to complete each day's schedule because of David's conduct on the set.

The tone of the counterproposal wasn't meant to be provocative, but neither was it conciliatory. It was a clear message from Steven: not only wouldn't he capitulate to the inflated demands the other side had put on the table; he also wouldn't stand for a repetition of the first season's morale problems.

Steven obviously had the law on his side—David's original contract was binding. But it was just as obvious that if David were to refuse to work, whatever the legal consequences to *him* might be, the show would be without its lead. So unless the other side believed he was bluffing and would eventually cave in, Steven's counterproposal also communicated his willingness to roll the dice on the ability of the show to survive David's absence.

Now David and his representatives had to decide what outcome they really wanted. David had a budding film career; we'd postponed our start date for the second season's shooting so that he could work in *Kiss of Death*, his first starring role in a feature. As rumors began circulating that his agents were testing the waters to see what feature roles David would be offered if he left the show and what sort of money he could command (of course, for them to have made such inquiries officially while David was under a binding contract would have been immoral and unethical and therefore unthinkable), David's representatives changed their negotiating stance: they wanted David released from *NYPD Blue*.

Steven didn't blink. He called me to his office and said he'd decided that whether or not the show survived without

David, life was too short for us to continue working with him. Once Steven had consulted with ABC, we'd determine a schedule for writing David out.

Not having been present at the conversation, I can only imagine the enthusiasm with which the network heads received Steven's news. After years of trying, they finally had a hit show on Tuesday night, which now gave every promise of going down the crapper. The network invested several days in back-channel efforts to effect a reconciliation, then finally accepted that it wasn't a question of whether David was going but when.

Resolving this question of when now became the misery of my existence. The episodes already written needed to be reconstructed, and time to rewrite them was extremely short; we were to begin shooting in less than a month. I needed to know the target episode for David's leaving, work backward in conceiving the appropriate story arc, then get the writing done.

But a slew of contingencies had to be resolved, the most important, of course, being casting. Steven never doubted which actor he was going to pursue; as he had two years ago when we'd first conceived *NYPD Blue*, he wanted Jimmy Smits. Jimmy would consider joining the show, but was shooting a film in Morocco, and the time difference and uncertain logistics of communication made the negotiating process even more of a protracted pain in the balls than usual.

As those discussions proceeded, Steven temporized with both the Caruso camp and the network. Because of a film role which had fortuitously presented itself, David's representatives wanted to limit the number of episodes he'd have to work in to two. Steven's position was that the minimum number of episodes we'd need to write Kelly out effectively was four. The network wanted his character to appear in the first eight. I wanted a decision before I cut someone's throat.

After two weeks of triangulated exchanges, the material terms of a contract with Jimmy had been essentially agreed on; what remained were stipulations and provisos presented by his representatives about the nature of the character he'd portray. Their natural concern was that in the process of orchestrating Kelly's departure, inadequate attention might be given to conceiving Jimmy's character and integrating him into the world of the show.

Finally, Steven and Jimmy had a two-person conversation during which Steven acknowledged the realities and limitations imposed by our time constraints. Steven said that no contract could guarantee what the results of our efforts would be in rendering Jimmy's character; all he could point to by way of assurance was the quality of work Jimmy and he had done together in the past.

Jimmy agreed to join the show. He said he wanted to take a little time off after finishing his project in Morocco. We asked if he could do that in New York, while getting to know Bill.

Second season cast of *NYPD Blue*
Used by permission of Capital Cities/ABC,
Inc.

chapter 12

In the entertainment community nothing stays a secret very long. The difficulty of our negotiations with David had quickly leaked to the media; so had the possibility David might leave. Still, the announcement confirming his departure brought a surge of public resentment. This was directed in some measure at Steven for failing to effectuate a compromise, but especially at David for what was perceived as greedy disloyalty.

The public's apportioning of blame had less to do with the merits of the situation than with David's visibility and the bond viewers forge with television characters. A relationship with John Kelly which had been deepening and growing was going to end, people didn't like it, and David was the most recognizable and emotionally accessible target.

It was also natural that David's imminent leaving would get more focus in the national press than Jimmy's prospectively joining the show several months in the future. But in New York City, where he'd just arrived from Morocco, Jimmy was surprised to be the object of an outpouring of interest and encouragement as, each day, the tabloids covered in multiple-page layouts the crash-course tutorial Bill was giving him in police work.

BILL HAD JIMMY SPEND time in precinct houses in Brooklyn and Queens. He took him out on cases, including the homicide of a Korean minister burned alive when thieves torched his church in the aftermath of a robbery. ("The guy didn't back off," Bill said about Jimmy later in a phone call to Los Angeles. "He stood it all right, and the DOA was burned pretty good.") Jimmy also spent hours at the shooting range to familiarize himself with handling various weapons (the last target he peppered that day with automatic-weapon fire hangs now in his trailer on the set).

Everywhere, cops made Jimmy welcome, from One Police Plaza in Manhattan, where Commissioner Bratten interrupted a meeting with department brass so each of the bosses could meet Jimmy and shake hands, to a street in Queens where a traffic cop had pulled Bill over for rolling through a stop sign. Bill's letting the traffic cop know he was on The Job was what kept the summons book in the cop's pocket, but it was Jimmy the cop wished good luck.

* * *

DAVID RETURNED TO WORK on *NYPD Blue* looking gaunt and haunted. He was so thin we worried he was ill, but were told he'd lost weight intentionally to look better on the larger screens of movie theaters.

There was sadness in David, even beneath the distant bravado he'd show moving from the set to his trailer in company with the bodyguard who was now his constant companion. David wanted to be a movie star, but I know in a large part of himself he regretted his coming separation, not from our show, but from the character of Kelly.

I've read interviews in which David said that he should not be confused with John Kelly, although Kelly represented qualities he was striving to attain. I can't count the times I watched that process of striving as David tormented himself (and others) in preparing a scene, then discovered in performance the humanity and compassion which eluded him in life. He had the stamina and will as an actor to fight through the impediments in his own nature which deprived him of the qualities he knew Kelly possessed. David had a world of guts; Kelly was a character he'd fought over and over again to become; and now he was going to lose him.

* * *

One thing a cop knows how to do in a courtroom is stick with his story. Before you get on the stand, you keep going over what you're going to say and make sure it's square with what people know happened. Then, when you're up there testifying, you stick to your guns. Anything they try, provoking you or so forth, you're a thick-headed Irishman, all you know is what you saw, your recollection is what it is.

This was Bill, explaining to me how Kelly would handle himself on the witness stand.

We're not talking about framing a guy. I wouldn't do that if my life depended on it. But there's ways and ways of telling how something happened, and if you know you're not screwing a person, you do what you have to to get your point across. I'd always go out of my way, when I'd give testimony where there was disagreement what happened in an interview prior to a skel confessing, I'd make sure I'd look the defendant square in the eye when I was saying what happened in there, so if he's sitting thinking, "This prick isn't saying what he did, getting me to confess," or so forth, I wanted the skel to know that both of us knew he was fucking guilty, and what was going to happen to him was just what he deserved.

That's how Kelly would be, with looking at the prosecutor when he was testifying. He'd look him right in the eye and say his version and that would be it.

We'd decided that Kelly would be driven from the force as a result of his efforts to protect Licalsi; not that he'd be caught in a lie, although he does lie to protect her, but that in the aftermath of testimony in which he acknowledged their personal relationship, and with Licalsi having confessed to murder, Kelly would become a public-relations liability to the department, and therefore its target.

Bill had explained that under such circumstances, the department wouldn't try to fire Kelly; rather it would disempower him, freeze him out of any meaningful position or responsibility. A cop like Kelly, Bill said, wouldn't stand for this. Recognizing the beginnings of the process of harassment and disenfranchisement, understanding its intention and eventual outcome, Kelly would preempt it. He'd quit.

WE TOLD THE STORY in four episodes. David's performance was understated and withheld, and the public had been so saturated with information about the why, when, and how of his leaving that the dramatic tension of the story line was pretty thoroughly undermined, but the ratings were very high and the episodes more or less well received critically.

The minority report was delivered by the television journalist Marvin Kitman of *Newsday*, who opined that we'd betrayed and prostituted Kelly's character in our portrayal of his leaving, that his actions weren't true to his nature. This thinking showed the same high quality as Kitman's prior effusions about the show.

While scrambling to construct the final Kelly episodes, Steven and I also talked about the new role Jimmy would play. I can probably best explain how we came to our sense of Bobby Simone's character through a brief digression.

The view which deprecates television as a storytelling medium points to the writer's need to honor an oppressive array of requirements foreign to the story itself. Considered the most onerous of these is the advertising sequence which obtrudes every fifteen minutes, along with its corollary requirement of a socko ending for the scene just prior to it which will bring the audience back.

I try to believe it's possible to serve two masters—for example, in accommodating the commercial break to conceive and offer stories whose dramatic structure naturally consists in four climactic events, and thereby to neutralize what's coercive and inimical in the Capitalist System to my Art.

We tried to take a similar (and maybe similarly self-deluding) approach—that is, serving two masters, trying to make organic and constructive a consideration which was originally extraneous—in thinking about the character of Simone. With nothing like the two years available we'd spent imagining John Kelly (shooting would begin on the first of Jimmy's episodes in two weeks), we tried to conceive of a character who would only permit himself to be known slowly and after shared experience had generated trust, whose life experience had left him emotionally foreclosed and inaccessible. In this way, by building into Simone's story arc natural obstacles to the quick bond we and viewers wanted to form, and natural premiums at the level of storytelling to these obstacles' overcoming, we tried to find a legitimate way to buy ourselves time.

One thing, I think this guy'd fly birds. Whatever you come up with, the bad that happened to him, he'd still have his pigeons.

Bill was trying hard to help, not just because he knew we were in trouble, but out of worry about the demands the show was making on my health.

Once, around this time, after he'd spent the weekend with us in California and I'd seemed tired to him, after he'd gotten on the red-eye and flown back to New York, and, according to his routine, was driving straight to the homicide squad in Queens to do an eight-to-four shift, Bill pulled off the road to call Los Angeles and find out how I'd slept.

"Bill," I said, "it's five o'clock in the fucking morning. I don't know yet how I slept."

Bill tried to protest that, with the three-hour time difference, where I was it had to be eleven, but he ran out of steam by the middle of his sentence. "Go to sleep," he said miserably, and hung up the phone.

But four or five times a day, at more sensible hours, he called with ideas.

One aspect, him breaking in with a partner's going to be no day at the beach. You get all kinds of difficulties.

I had one partner, Henny Heinsohn; what broke us up was his conduct in restaurants. Every restaurant we'd go to, this guy went ten rounds with the menu. And we're not talking about complicated menus. And the places we'd eat, no one's leaving the waitresses any ten-dollar bills. They make their living off volume. So someone sits looking at a menu ten minutes, they're not too thrilled.

But what was the most aggravating, with all the studying, Henny always ordered brisket or a meatball sub. So it used to drive me nuts, watching him stare at the menu, and the waitress doing a slow burn, and knowing where we were going with his selection.

I was a young detective then, and a guy had told me to partner with Henny because he had twenty-five years and could show me the ropes, but with a few months of lunches I had enough.

Bill also told me about Chris Dowdell, whom he'd part-nered with for years, and whom I came to know as a friend.

Even Chris, any reason he'd feel somehow you'd loused up the catching order, the sequence we'd draw cases to work on, if he'd feel he'd drawn a stinky one 'cause you'd caught a case out of order, he could do a burn for three months. Now eight and ten hours a day you're riding in a car with a guy won't talk to you, and can't either of you remember what the hell he's mad about.

Another guy, Paddy Nugent—they used to call him Little Dutch Boy 'cause once he chased a perp into a paint store, shot up about forty Dutch Boy paint statues in the store base-ment. Paddy was about six-four, two-eighty, arms maybe twice the size of your thighs. A nice guy, but with three drinks he absolutely needed a straitjacket, and who could put it on him?

His idea of fun, shit-faced?—a guy shooting pool, a com-pletely strange bar, the Dutch Boy'd get up and piss on his leg. The guy's bent over his shot at the pool table, all of a sudden he feels his leg getting wet, there's Paddy pissing on him. Now the place goes up for grabs, you're in a strange bar, you've got to fight an hour and a half.

Another great piece of humor, all his top teeth were gone, Paddy'd walk along the bar dunking his upper plate in peo-ple's drinks. That always brought out great friendliness. And as big as he was, Paddy wasn't that great of a fighter. He'd go, but he'd always need help. So you'd wind up hooking-and-jabbing with guys to stand up for him, and he'd dunked his teeth in their drinks.

"Anyways," Bill said, "maybe you could use some of that."

I told him we could use it all.

"How does Steven stand with the birds?"

"The birds are in. The new guy raises pigeons."

"Yeah, 'cause the neighborhood he probably grew up, not running with a gang, or you weren't some type of shut-in, generally you'd be on the roofs."

SANTAYANA ONCE SUGGESTED THAT the seeds of America's mistrust of highbrows were planted at the first American universities, which espoused the Calvinist view of life as full of suffering and uncertainty. This was so at variance with the success that students usually went on to experience as adults in nineteenth century America that while in later life they might pay lip service to the importance of diplomas and higher learning, in their hearts they respected neither.

We thought that maybe Simone had grown up on mean streets, but in a loving family; that out of their own ex-

perience his parents had taught him to view life as a struggle portioned with sorrow—but that he might have lived
into his late twenties without himself having suffered loss.
If he'd been successful both professionally (fast-tracked
to his gold shield because he was not only a good cop but
a minority) and personally (marrying his first love, the first
girl he'd ever slept with as a high school senior at seventeen), then whatever he professed both out of respect
for his parents' teaching and because of what he'd seen as
a cop, in his secret heart he might not believe that suffering was ever for *him*. For this person to have his wife come
home from work one afternoon saying she'd been to a doctor who'd found she was ill; to have to watch, unable to
offer relief, the sudden onset of a suffering at the end of
which death was release, might bring not only sadness but
an embitterment kept silent out of the private knowledge
that it was petulant and unfair; supposedly, he'd always
known this could happen.

Time would find out what he could learn. If he could
truly love life, knowing now what it could do, life would
bring him out again. But it would happen slowly.

Sipowitz offers advice to rookie
detective James Martinez
(Nicholas Turturro).
*Used by permission of Capital
Cities/ABC, Inc.*

chapter 13

NYPD Blue broke *Hill Street*'s record with twenty-six Emmy nominations for the 1993–1994 season, including all the nominations for writing. Both Dennis and David were nominated for best actor, after my campaign to dissuade Dennis from letting himself be entered in this category proved fruitless. As a practical matter, I'd thought David was a shoo-in—every journal with an opinion had named him the likely winner—and that Dennis would be too, for supporting actor, if he'd let his representatives submit him for it. Dennis said that, win or lose, he wanted to be up for the right award.

Dennis isn't a combative soul, although he has enormous pride. He cares about his work, and about sustaining the balance of his life away from it. At the beginning of our first season, after David's outburst during the shooting of their locker-room scene, Dennis had insisted they have a conversation which would amount to a working out of ground rules. They did meet, David offered enough of an apology to get the locker-room incident off the table, and something like a civil tone was established between them.

For the rest of the year, they barely spoke. When David "went off," it tended not to be in Dennis's presence. When it was, Dennis walked away from him.

To the credit of both, the distance between Dennis and David didn't read on film—the Kelly-Sipowicz relationship remained successful as the emotional center of the show.

But after the first sequence of episodes, as we did with Kelly, we began to widen the viewer's exposure to Sipowicz's past and his personal relationships. The relationship list wasn't long. As a longtime drunk, Sipowicz had burned most of his bridges. But after having been shot, and the enforced drying out of a hospital convalescence, we were able to show him slowly feeling his way into sobriety.

He initiated a hesitant and uncertain personal relationship with the female assistant district attorney he'd first been seen insulting. He even made a gesture at helping the son who hadn't spoken to him in five years, although this effort (letting Andy Jr. know the girl with whom he was in love was unfaithful and already pregnant) ended disastrously. Throughout, Dennis portrayed with discomfited dignity a man refusing to yield to self-pity as he addresses the mess he has made of his life and counts the cost of time lost.

A NUMBER OF ARTICLES have been written (I don't know how many have been read) about similarities between my personality and Sipowicz's. It's been proposed that when provoked we share traits such as abrasiveness and an impulse to verbal abuse. Also like Sipowicz, for a long time I was an active addict, although I was more of a plural offender.

Except to the extent I reenact certain aspects of my father's nature, I think it's closer to the truth to say Sipowicz's personality is more like my dad's.

Last night, as I was thinking about doing this writing, I remembered two incidents at the same greasy spoon where my family ate supper every Thursday and Sunday night (my dad being a creature of unbreakable habits) which suggest the dimension and poles of my father's nature.

The diner was called the Your Host, and it was part of a small local chain. It's an index of how *much* a creature of habit my father was that in the course of our drive to the restaurant we would pass two other Your Hosts—the Your Host which was our destination was around the corner from the hospital where my dad was chief of surgery, and knew how to prepare his steak-and-melted-cheese sandwich.

In the first incident, either before we left for the restaurant or while we were in the car, I did something that made him mad. It wasn't intentional, because I never tried to get my father mad my whole life. Maybe I'd been late getting home from playing with friends or somehow else loused up the process of our getting to the diner. Also, I'm sure he'd come home frustrated or upset about something from work so whatever I did was magnified as an irritant.

My dad held the door as my brother and mother went into the diner. As I followed them inside, moving under his arm, he brought his fist down on the back of my neck. I was eight or nine, and besides the pain of being hit I couldn't understand what was going on. Nothing that happened through the rest of the meal explained it to me. My dad didn't give any indication the event had taken place except to sit with the muscles in his jaws working, which was a sign he was upset. I didn't say anything either.

In one way this incident wasn't typical—my dad hit me three times in my life. But he *was* always driven by things it was hard to understand, and which seemed to force him to live in a very narrow and specific way, and you didn't want to mess him up.

My dad and I never made any more reference to what happened going into the Your Host, although late that night as I was trying to go to sleep, he came into my room and rubbed my hair.

The other incident at the diner involved a book salesman with cerebral palsy whom my father had operated on for stomach cancer. Patients were always coming up to my father at the restaurant. They liked him not just because they were grateful for the outcome of their operation, but also because he had some instinctive sense of how to get people back on their feet emotionally after their surgery; he'd play on an older woman's vanity or a middle-aged man's desire to get back to work or get even with someone or to prove again he was sexually capable. As recently as a year ago (my father's been dead for fifteen years), a woman of forty came up to me in the studio commissary at Twentieth Century–Fox and asked if I was related to a surgeon from Buffalo who had my same last name. When I said that was my father, the woman took my hands between hers and told me how when she was a girl of fifteen she'd been operated on for a malignancy and afterward had been in despair not only because she was afraid of her cancer spreading but because now she had a disfiguring surgical scar on her belly. The morning she was to leave the hospital my dad had come into her room and taken her hands between his and told her he promised her she was cured, and that she was a beautiful girl, not to worry about her scar because it was a time-saver, it would only rule out the jerks.

The book salesman who had cerebral palsy had difficulty managing his samples as he moved to the diner's counter, but when he saw my father in the booth his eyes got bright and his mouth shaped into a crooked smile and with his knees knocking together and his hands locked at the wrists like hooks he came over to the booth. It was hard to make out his exact words because his palsy impaired his speech, but it was clear he was introducing himself and was pleased to meet my father's family.

After he'd gone back to the counter and given the waitress his order (the salesman was a regular too), the waitress brought Cokes to the table for me and my brother. At the counter, the book salesman raised a claw-hand in salutation to indicate he'd sent them over.

I was worried about him paying for our Cokes. I knew he couldn't be making much money. I asked my dad if there wasn't some way we could pay for them instead. "You let him pay," my dad said quietly.

MY DAD'S MOTHER WAS the eldest of nine children. *Her* mother had died shortly after my grandparents' marriage. With her new husband, my grandmother moved back into her parents' house to take care of her widowed father and her younger brothers and sisters. My dad was born and grew up in this house with his eight aunts and uncles (my grandmother was diabetic; all her other pregnancies ended in stillbirths).

A number of these uncles, my great-uncles, wound up in the rackets (one of them, my Great-uncle Nate, managed the Latin Quarter in partnership with Lou Walters, Barbara Walters's father), but because my father was of the next generation the plan was for him to attend college and follow a more reputable course. My father once told me how when he was a teenager and shooting pool on Williams Street, one of his uncles came into the pool hall, grabbed my father's companion by the hair, and threw him through the window to discourage him from leading my dad into idle pastimes.

My dad did go to college, and to medical school, and he became a surgeon of distinction—a clinical professor who conducted some of the early experiments in vascular surgery on dogs (some of the survivors became our household pets), and later perfected several techniques in the gastrointestinal surgery which became his specialty.

But he always was drawn to his uncles' way of life. In August, as a college student, he'd go to Saratoga to earn tuition money as a busboy at the Piping Rock Casino, which my Uncle Natey was managing for Meyer Lansky. Later, when he'd entered private practice, he maintained a 10 percent participation in the bookmaking operation of my Uncle Haskell. From the time I was seven, it was my job to write down the bets my uncle would call and cryptically recite into the telephone. Always, since he was booking these bets, my dad, Uncle Haskell, and I were to pull for the team opposite the one I'd inscribed.

I was six when my dad first took me to Saratoga. By this time he had quite a successful practice and had bought a few claiming horses (owning racehorses was something none of his uncles ever attained). We sat together all day, first at the luncheon table, where the waiter kept two shots of scotch in ritual position in anticipation of my dad's arrival (the rest of the year getting my dad's scotch ready was my job), then in the box, where through the rest of the day we watched the races and people came by to see him (at the track everyone called him the Doc). I met Vic Gilardi that day, the agent for the great jockey Jorge Velasquez. Vic stopped to consult with my dad in a bullfrog voice about the jockey Velasquez's shoulder problem. Sol Rutchick, who trained my dad's few horses, and whose fate was to be remembered as the only trainer not to be at Churchill Downs when his horse won the Kentucky Derby, came by with a tip on a horse he trained for Abe Chait.

Alleged to manage the thugs who slowed unionization of the garment industry, Chait weighed more than 350 pounds and was a hypochondriac obsessive-compulsive who refused to touch used money; he was devoted to my dad, and once gave him a racehorse as a Christmas present. (A few years later, Track Security came to Chait's box at Saratoga and forced him to leave the grounds, having suddenly made the discovery he was a felon; in fact, Chait, who was trying to buy a secret piece of Yonkers Raceway, was being sent a message by a recalcitrant assemblyman. When his father was taken from the track, Chait's twenty-three-year-old son remained in the family's box and bet on the remainder of the racing card; for the rest of his life, when my dad saw Chait's son, he would turn away and refuse to speak to him because when his father had been taken away, the son hadn't walked out as well.)

I also met Slim Sully, Sol Rutchick's assistant trainer. When Rutchick had refused to indulge the whim of Jack Amiel (the money backer of Jack Dempsey's Restaurant) by sending to Kentucky a horse Rutchick was sure had no chance to win, it was Slim who was dispatched to saddle Count Turf for the Kentucky Derby, and watched him win under the magnificent ride of the dwarf jockey Conn McCreary.

I remember, on my first day at the track, my dad slipping me a $20 bill and whispering to me, since I was not permitted at the windows, that Max the waiter would run my bets. I won three of the nine races, but I kept all the tickets.

As we left together that day, my dad said he didn't want to hear about me sneaking out to such places on my own.

* * *

TWO YEARS BEFORE I was born, when he was in military service during the Second World War, my dad was in a terrible auto accident. He and my mother had been married less than a year. My brother Bob had just been born. My dad had enlisted in the physicians' unit formed by his hospital, and had been scheduled to go overseas the next morning. That night, a jeep he was driving was hit by a transport truck. He was crushed from the midsection down. I've seen a photograph in a textbook on traumatic injuries which shows an X ray taken when my dad was first admitted to the hospital—his bladder can be visualized about four inches below his neck.

I've never known the full story of how my father came to be in the jeep. The public version was that the base was sealed down because of the imminent troop embarcation and he'd taken the jeep to drive into town to call my mother and tell her goodbye.

Over the next year my dad endured a series of reconstructive operations—even later in life, every three months he'd need to be catheterized to dilate his urinary passage, which was constricted by scar tissue. Throughout this time, he was dosed with narcotics to manage his pain.

It was several months before he'd let my mother come into the hospital room. Finally, though, he did allow her to see him, and eventually to spend time with him in the room. When he was released from the hospital, they left together to get Bob. By this time, my mother was pregnant with me.

IN THE MIDDLE OF my own life, after more than a decade of heroin addiction, I signed myself into a rehab unit. For a number of days, as I went through withdrawal, I wouldn't see the facility psychiatrist. After about a week, when I was at lunch, which at this point was an adventurous experience, the psychiatrist came up to me in the hospital cafeteria. He said that if I was going to have any hope for a sustained sobriety it wasn't enough to kick; I'd have to attempt an emotional recovery as well. Later, after we'd talked a little while, I found myself crying, saying I was afraid if I got involved with this I was going to lose my love for my father.

I don't have enough distance to write well about any of this. What I'm laboring to say is that, insofar as there are similarities between my dad and Sipowicz, I'm grateful to have had the chance to portray Sipowicz's character; to show him in what another writer called his "obstinate finality"—that is, in full human complication: to do him justice.

I'D MADE A GOOD income from the time I'd begun writing for television, but at the point that Steven left *Hill Street* in 1986, the keepers of the flame at MTM began paying me a *lot* of money. Beyond being moved to express appreciation for my work, they may also have been concerned to ensure that, with Steven gone, their stock of episodes for syndication would keep growing. There may also have been a further purpose: they were trying to entice some British investors into buying the company lock, stock, and library; *Hill Street* as a going concern was a high-profile asset.

I've already acknowledged I didn't squirrel much of this money away. I used most of it to buy racehorses.

In August 1986, I had one of these horses shipped back to New York to run at Saratoga. Horses my dad had owned had won races at other New York tracks, but never there, where he could see it. I had my dad's racing colors reactivated, and when the horse, whose name was El Mansour, came onto the track for the post parade, the jockey, Jorge Velasquez, was wearing my father's silks.

Even though my dad died in 1979, and there was no one in my family left to go, I'd kept up payments on his racing box, and made it available to the dwindling group of his surviving cronies.

That day in August, as I sat in the box and watched El Mansour win, I wanted to feel I'd closed a chapter for my dad or myself or my memories of him.

Instead, I felt like someone who'd tried to buy something that wasn't for sale, like one of those people my dad would sometimes point to when I'd be with him at Saratoga as a boy. The person might be flashing a fistful of high-denominated winning tickets, or being boisterous on the way to the winners circle, or parading a showgirl companion. "That's a phony," my dad would say.

AT THE EMMYS, WHEN Dennis won for his portrayal of Sipowicz, *that* felt really good.

Dennis Franz and his wife, Joanie,
Jimmy Smits, and Bill joined Stephen
Bochco for a trip to the Super Bowl.
David stayed at home to work.

chapter 14

My Uncle Haskell used to say some of the best boxing matches he'd ever seen were fixed (and he had reason to know which these were). He explained that if the boxers had ability and didn't want to lose their licenses, they worked hard to make the fight look real.

Jimmy and Dennis worked like that together. They were good friends, but as actors brought off wonderfully the wary getting-to-know-each-other of two men who were proudly professional but, for different reasons, emotionally isolated.

Sipowicz, more openly irascible and encrusted by habit, tolerates no more than a handshake and greeting from Simone before letting their boss know the partnership is doomed. When Fancy asks what Simone has done to provoke him, Sipowicz answers emphatically, "Don't get me started. It's a whole attitude. 'How you doin'?,' this type of thing."

Fancy doesn't get it. "He asked you how you were doing?"

Sipowicz is saved from further explanation by a crime call coming in.

Working their first case, Simone and Sipowicz bump into each other's interrogation techniques, out of phase even as to the point at which a suspect should be offered a soft drink (feeling Simone has been too indulgent, Sipowicz observes, "I generally like 'em to give something up before I cater their lunch"). Even at the end of the shift, when Simone has invited the detectives on the day tour out for a beer, Sipowicz counters Simone's information that he's a pigeon flier with an analysis of pigeons' shortcomings compared to the tropical fish Sipowicz raises:

"I got a clown-fish couple just had eggs. In the morning while I'm having coffee that male cleans each egg with his mouth. He never breaks one. The whole day while I'm working, him and the wife guard that nest and fan water over their eggs. Those are dedicated fish."

Sipowicz considers Simone with satisfaction. "You see that kind of thing in pigeons?"

* * *

THE RATINGS FOR JIMMY'S first episode were among the highest we ever got, and his reviews were uniformly positive. Even those critics who were sullen about David's departure absolved him from their displeasure with the show.

Jimmy himself is a perfectionist and wasn't satisfied with his performance. It also took a particular emotional discipline for him to accept our approach to the character—a lesser actor (and person) would have been afraid the audience and critics would misinterpret Simone's chosen stoicism simply to be a lack of inwardness. Our appreciation of Jimmy's bravery compounded our pleasure as we watched his character open and grow.

As I write this, Emmy nominations for the second season have been announced, but not the winners. Both Dennis and Jimmy are nominees. Last week, Dennis, who'd been out of town, returned my congratulatory call.

"I'll tell you the absolute truth," he said. "If Jimmy wins it, I'd be just as glad as if it's me."

"Just like last year," I said.

"Yeah," Dennis said. "Just."

OCTOBER 1, 1994, WAS the date Bill's police pension would be fully vested. He'd set this as his target date for leaving The Job, moving to California, and coming to work on the show full-time.

Many of his friends worried if it was the right thing for Bill to do. Bill had retired once before, in the mid-eighties, to manage the security affairs of a real-estate mogul. He'd lasted six months.

I was friends with a guy from when I worked as a bouncer at P.J. Clarke's. The guy used to get oiled up and come in with bad women, and I tried to look out for him, let the women know I didn't want to find him rolled behind a mickey and walking around Central Park in his underwear thinking he was Herbert Hoover. The guy was friends with this real-estate guy, and liked me well enough, when he heard about the security job being available, he told the guy he should talk to me.

The interview went good, and the guy offered me the job at a bump from what I was making as a detective. With my department pension it'd mean doubling what I earned. I was just divorced, and I'd been glad enough to give my family my money and commit to support, but I was broke.

I remember telling Stanley Strull, my partner at the time, that I loved our Job but I was forty-five years old and I didn't have ten cents and I had to make a practical decision.

Anyways, I accepted the offer. This man had been polite in the interview, but when I went to work he turned out to have bad manners—he'd order you around like a coolie. I was in charge of security for four skyscraper apartment buildings in Manhattan plus homes he had in Connecticut and on the East Side and out on Long Island and also a fleet of cars. It wasn't a job where you'd pick up in twenty minutes how to do everything right, but it seemed like this guy started yelling at me the first day I walked through the door.

Plus he was miserable to drive with, no matter what route you took he'd yell it was wrong, and the one time a week he'd drive with me as a passenger, which was when he'd go to his psychiatrist, he was always starting fights with other drivers where I'd wind up having to get out of the car to calm things down. Plus he had a nut-case sister who lived in one of his buildings who kept being bombarded by Venusian thought-rays all hours of the day and night and by her neighbors trying to sneak in and assault her or by their having a campaign to drive her crazy with Oldies music. She was a full-time job her-self.

The man's offices were on West 57th, and the first weeks af-ter I started I'd be miserable going up the elevator 'cause I knew when the door opened I'd be at work. Then it got where I'd be miserable just waking up, 'cause I knew once I got out of bed and had breakfast, work was next. About a month into this job, I couldn't get to sleep anymore 'cause I knew next thing I'd wake up and then it'd be work and get yelled at by this man and listen to the planetary report from his sister.

I'd known Commissioner Kelly both from The Job and because both of us were in the military reserves after we'd served in

Vietnam. I finally called him up. I said that I knew once you were retired the door was closed but I was miserable and wanted to come back. The commissioner said let him look into it. A little while later he called me back and said it would take some time to get the paperwork taken care of but it would turn out all right.

I gave my two weeks' notice that same day. Even though I'd bent over backwards being polite to this man, afterward he told our mutual friend who'd recommended me to him he was just as glad I'd quit because three or four times I'd looked at him like I was going to kill him.

It was three more months, but finally I got my job back.

BILL MET JIMMY BRESLIN when Bill was working the Son of Sam case and the psychopath David Berkowitz was sending Jimmy letters. Jimmy has written many columns about Bill in the years since, about cases Bill's worked but also about his dealings with his dogs, cats, finches, cockatiels, and talking parrots. (One of the parrots, an African gray named Smokey, says "Call the cops," "*NYPD Blue*—great show," and every conceivable obscenity with an emphasis and conviction so like Bill's that with your back turned it's hard to know whose Brooklyn accents you're listening to.)

Jimmy dealt with Bill during his real-estate period. He had big reservations about Bill's retirement idea.

Jimmy had formed a good enough opinion of me not to subscribe to the usual argument against Bill's joining us full-time, which was that we'd eat Bill's stories up and then spit him out. "You're a first-grade detective," he told Bill. "That's not just a title. It's who you are. Walk away from that, you're going to hate waking up again."

I did my best to make an objective assessment for Bill of what his prospects would be if he went to work for us full-time. The audience clearly was accepting Jimmy's character. Assuming none of its key pieces was dislodged, *NYPD Blue* would run a number of years. While it was on the air, Bill would make a good income, and after that, as long as I was active, I would work with him on other projects.

I pointed out that, having lived through our troubles with David Caruso, Bill would understand that key pieces *could* be dislodged. There could be contract disputes, or accidents. He knew my health was uncertain, and that a time could come when I wasn't able to be active and work with him. In making his choice, he had to recognize the small but real possibility he could wind up out of a job.

I suggested he could weigh his choices from a purely financial perspective by estimating how long he'd need to work on *NYPD Blue* to make the same amount of money he'd make by staying on The Job ten more years, which was the longest Bill figured he'd stay a detective anyway.

In our first season Bill's title had been technical adviser, and I'd supplemented the relatively modest salary he'd received from Steven's company. Four months before, at the beginning of our second season, he'd been promoted to consulting producer, and his salary approximated an entry-level writer's (in our business such writers are called story editors), which was better than he'd been doing with the real estate man. As long as the show ran, he could expect comfortable yearly raises. Assuming these raises, we worked it out that if the show lasted three years, no matter what happened thereafter, in terms of money Bill would be ahead of the game.

I told Bill the cards now were faceup. When he asked what I thought he should do, I said I didn't want to be part of his decision. In terms of his worth to the show, it was a fifty-fifty call; it would be great to have him with me all the time so we could work on stories, but in terms of maintaining his contacts and access to cases, he might be more valuable staying on The Job.

I told him he shouldn't be thinking about what was good for the show or anyone else. My concern as his friend was that he not move out to Los Angeles and feel that he'd lost himself.

Bill was always uncertain whether he had any standing with the show apart from his relationship with me. The short version was, he worried how he stood with Steven.

Steven now made a gesture which was not only generous but touched a deep chord in Bill's nature: if Bill moved, he could live in a home Steven owned in nearby Rustic Canyon. The house had three bedrooms, so Bill's daughters could stay with him when they came for visits. Its backyard was terraced into a hillside and full of greenery. There would be room for Bill's dog and cat and all his birds.

In Bill's mind, Steven's offer tipped the scales. He said October 1, 1994, would definitely be it. He wouldn't officially retire until December 31, but with his accumulated leave time, he would work his last eight-to-four on the final day of September.

BILL WORKED TWO HOMICIDE cases during what he'd said would be his final two weeks as an active detective.

One of these was a multiple homicide in which the two victims had been tied up with stockings and stabbed more than eighty times. The victims were a black male and female in their mid-thirties. They'd been murdered in a housing project where many residents were crack users, and the female victim was known to use the drug. She was separated from her husband, and on Saturdays, because this was the day their mother most often tended to use crack, her oldest son would take her youngest daughter, the only child who still lived with the mother, to stay at their grandmother's house. It was the son who had found his mother and the male victim murdered when he brought his sister home the following morning.

Bill originally went at the homicides as a case of mistaken identity (he'd been able to rule out the woman's former husband as a suspect—the man had moved South). On Saturday nights at this project during the warm weather the tenants tended to leave their doors open and move from apartment to apartment. People would be high and confused and pair off casually with strangers. Often, female tenants would exchange sex for crack, sometimes going out on the street to buy the drug while the male waited in the apartment. (Crack is sometimes called rock, and these women were nick-named "rock stars.") A male who was partying with the woman who lived next door to the victim had given the woman money to go out and cop and was furious when she hadn't come back. He was already high, and after pacing up and down the walkway awhile shouting for the missing woman, he went out on the street to find her. A number of the apartment residents theorized that he'd come back to the wrong apartment, forgotten what his companion looked like (he'd only met her that night), and killed her along with the man whose high and sex he believed had been bought with his money.

We found this guy and I talked to him a good while, but I wound up not liking him for the homicides. He did have a record, but almost everyone we talked to from that building had a record, and he stood the questioning pretty good.

Later that day, we got to the girl who'd taken this guy off for his money. We made her understand we weren't looking to jam her for anything she'd been doing, all we wanted was to clear these homicides. She gave up some names of different guys she'd seen on the floor that night walking from apartment to apartment and also people she'd seen on the street just outside the project.

One of the names she gave us was a guy she called Flowers. Along with all the other names, we ran Flowers through BCI as a last name and a first name and a nickname, but zeroed out for anyone from that area.

Another guy she'd talked about seeing on the street wasn't much of a candidate because no one from the building mentioned seeing him inside. But in the process of tracking all these people down, we grabbed the guy up. He turned out to be a parole violator. He mentioned this guy Flowers too, that he'd been with him and Flowers was all messed up and had gone in the building, and he knew Flowers had done a lot of time and was a strange guy.

I told this guy what I'd told the girl who lives next door to the DOAs—I wasn't looking to hurt him for anything else, if he helped me on this, I wouldn't violate him on his parole. He said he thought maybe he knew where Flowers stayed, he lived with some type of old relative who had the first floor of a house.

We drove around the neighborhood with him, and after about half an hour he pointed out a house about nine blocks from the projects where the homicides happened and said he thought that was where the guy we wanted lived. The house had a garden all manicured and with beautiful flowers in it. I felt like a dope not connecting his nickname Flowers with the possibility the guy gardened.

We kept the parole violator with us while we staked the place out and waited for Flowers to come back. After a while the violator needed to relieve himself, and I took him a few blocks to a commercial street and took him inside a coffee shop. When we were leaving, he pushed my arm and told me Flowers was across the street with two other guys.

All three of these guys were dressed in white. They looked like Good Humor men. They went into a bodega. I called the two detectives I was working with and they came where I was. We were trying to figure the best way to take this guy, and finally I just decided to go after him in the bodega.

He was at the counter and the two others were down an aisle. I grabbed him and put my gun to him. He had a .38 automatic stuck inside his shirt, and I was afraid his buddies might be packing too, but they turned out not to give me any trouble and I got him out of there.

I wound up feeling sorry for this Flowers. I talked to him a long time getting him to give up what happened.

We started out where he denied anything to do with the homicides, he said he thought he was in trouble because he was a convict in possession of a gun. We worked with that awhile. He talked about how much effort he put into staying out of trouble the two and a half years he'd been out, how he held two jobs to keep his mind right, working every day of the week and working in his grandmother's garden and only having the gun because of how the neighborhood was. I said I understood that. I was a homicide detective, we had two homicides to clear at the projects, and he'd been mentioned being there. If he could help us with the homicides, maybe the gun problem could go away.

Flowers said he'd been at the projects that night but he didn't know anything about the murders. He talked about all the doors being open on the long walkway, like it was the tier of a cellblock. He told me about the rock stars.

He had a bandage on the middle finger of one hand. He said he'd cut his hand gardening. I asked if I could see the cut.

It was exactly the cut someone gets on his finger when he's stabbing someone over and over and his hand gets covered with the victim's blood and the blood makes the knife handle slippery and finally the perpetrator's hand slides up the knife from slipping on the blood and gets cut on the knife blade. I told Flowers I'd seen a lot of cut hands like this and how most of those cuts happened.

He was a bad asthmatic and having a lot of trouble breathing. Believe it or not, he wanted a cigarette, he said that was the only thing calmed his chest down. I got him a cigarette, and he smoked it and then he told me what happened.

He told me he'd been smoking crack and sharing it with the woman he wound up killing, that he'd thought they were going to have sex and then this other guy came in—the male victim was a postal employee who'd dated the female victim a few times and who no one in the projects much liked—and the guy who'd walked in had talked to him like a punk.

Flowers said he wasn't sure who the woman preferred, he thought actually she probably preferred him and he should have kept himself under control and things would have been all right, but he got excited and pulled his gun on the guy, and then the woman started screaming and then he got afraid. He gagged both of them and tied them up, and then he knew he should've left but then he was upset that they could identify him, he'd worked so hard to keep his life together and now he'd wind up back in jail, in this one minute he'd blown everything, and so he got a knife and started stabbing them, and every time he put the blade into them he got more and more upset about now having ruined everything and that made him keep stabbing.

Bill was as happy as I've ever heard him the night he called and told me about grabbing Flowers up and Flowers having gone for the homicides. Michael Daly called me that same night and said Bill was crazy, fifty years old and going into that bodega with no bulletproof vest.

Two days after his arrest, Flowers died in his cell on Rikers Island of an asthma attack. When we'd talk on the phone, Bill kept coming back to Flowers and his death. In a way he felt sorry for the guy—he had a whole history of emotional disturbance, and the first time when he'd gone away for armed robbery when he was seventeen years old it had looked to Bill like a bogus charge. Also, Bill grows flowers, and that may have been another reason for his sympathy. But he was proud of having cleared the case.

"If that had to be the last one, I worked it pretty good," he said.

THE SECOND CASE INVOLVED a homicide in a gay bar. The owners of the bar were an uncle and nephew. The nephew was found in the bar's basement office, bound and gagged and shot in the back; there was some question as to whether death resulted from the bullet or the victim's having aspirated vomit into his lungs after being shot.

The homicide was discovered around three in the morning by a busboy, who ran upstairs and got the victim's uncle and the manager and one of the bouncers, all of whom rushed downstairs. The bouncer administered mouth-to-mouth resuscitation, but the victim didn't revive.

Bill questioned the co-owner uncle from six in the morning into the night and wound up convinced the uncle wasn't involved. He thought he might have a possible suspect in the owner of an Italian restaurant in which the uncle and nephew had invested, and who felt they were using their investment to elbow him out. Bill didn't think the restaurant owner had committed the crime, but did think he might have had something to do with commissioning it.

For the perpetrator, Bill was looking at the bouncer who'd come downstairs with the uncle and found the body.

For one thing, that busboy ran upstairs and told these people that kid was dead. Not shot, dead. And here comes the uncle and the manager and this bouncer downstairs, the bouncer tears the gag off the DOA's mouth, puke comes pouring out, and this guy tries resuscitation. That's a little big for me. That's a heroic dope or someone selling what a great guy he is who'd never be involved in a crime.

Bill called me every few hours as he worked the case. He was playing the bouncer slowly, giving no sign he was looking at him as a suspect.

I'm having him explain this place to me, who's hitting who in the seat. Then everyone he tells me about, I bring them in and talk to them off the angle the bouncer gave me, so when they go back and talk to the bouncer, he figures he's leading me around by the nose. And if I turn out wrong, at least I'm working through all the people, maybe I'll come up with something else.

One of the bar employees Bill questioned worked in the coat-check room, which had a view of the stairs leading into the basement. (Since the perpetrator had come in through a door in the basement which was always locked, Bill was sure someone who worked in the bar and had access to the basement had to have been involved in opening the door to the intruder.) The coat-check employee insisted he had seen no one go down the stairs all evening.

The bouncer had elliptically suggested to Bill that the coat-check employee might be protecting his boyfriend, who had been in the bar that evening, and whom the bouncer thought he might have seen coming up the stairs at the approximate time of the crime.

Maybe I'm gonna catch a break on the boyfriend.

Bill said this a few nights later, with a return of some of the optimism I'd noted leaking out of his voice.

I go to talk to him and he's checked himself into the happy farm. Maybe he's got a guilty mind.

A few days later, this lead fizzled out. The coat-check man's boyfriend checked out of the mental hospital and came in for an interview. Although he was pretty heavily sedated, the boyfriend persuaded Bill he hadn't been involved.

I gotta move on this bouncer.

Bill's approach, playing thickheaded Irish cop, was to tell the bouncer he'd been so swamped with competing information and versions of who was where when that he was asking a lot of people to take polygraphs. The bouncer agreed to take a lie-detector test.

That night I called Bill. I'd known the bouncer had taken the polygraph in the afternoon and was eager to hear how he'd done.

Bill was morose.

No fucking good.

"The guy passed?"

No, he flunked. But I couldn't move him afterward. I told him the polygraph was evidence, he'd been revealed lying, he'd better get in front. I went with the robbery-went-wrong, he'd never meant for violence to happen. I went with a lower charge for cooperation if he'd give up the guy put him up to it. I went with remorse. The guy went for the phone. He law-yered up. I'm screwed.

Bill kept working to find some lead in the web of promiscu-ous relationships among the bar's customers and employ-ees. He reinterviewed the manager, and a second bouncer, and the owner of the Italian restaurant. He repeatedly spoke to the victim's uncle. Nothing came of any of it.

On the phone, he sounded like someone with a chronic illness. His voice was distant and subdued.

October 1 was a few days away. I waited for the con-versation I knew was coming, when Bill would say he had to work the case a little while longer, until he had something to go at the bouncer with, or that he couldn't leave The Job off a case that didn't clear.

Bill called late on the night of September 29. His voice wasn't firm, but it was emphatic.

"A lot of guys can do this Job," he said. "Tomorrow, I'm going to do an eight-to-four, and then I'm getting on the fucking plane."

IN THE EPISODE WE did suggested by the gay bar murder case, Simone and Sipowicz collar the Italian restaurant owner for the crime. In real life, the restaurant owner is not a suspect (nor was the nephew, as we'd portrayed him, gay), and the case has never been solved.

But Bill did what he said he would. On September 30, he worked his last shift as an active detective, took a cab to the airport (he'd given his car to his daughter Jennifer), and got on the plane.

On his daily call the next morning, Jimmy Breslin's voice rasped into my telephone.

"He's your problem now," Jimmy said, then, with his usual Old World formality, hung up the phone in my ear.

Sipowitz and Fancy (James McDaniel) in
the 15th Precinct "meeting" room *Used
by permission of Capital Cities/ABC, Inc.*

chapter 15

While Bill was deciding about moving to California, I tried to navigate the shitstorm created by a talk I'd given to some aspiring writers. The talk was part of a monthly series sponsored by the Paulist Fathers of the Catholic Church and given by winners of the Humanitas Prize.

The topic I'd been assigned was "The Challenges and Pitfalls of Portraying Human Values in Entertainment Writing," which hadn't prompted in me any impulse to a comprehensive statement, so I'd suggested the audience ask questions and I'd try to answer. The session lasted four hours, and I thought it went well. But answers I'd given to several different questions at different points in the talk turned out to have had an aggregate effect of pissing some people off.

At one point I was asked about how I wrote the character of Sipowicz. I tried to describe the writer's process of synthesizing aspects of his own nature and of personalities he's observed into a credible character.

I was asked about Sipowicz's racism. I explained Steven's and my belief that *not* to portray racists in a series about New York cops would have made the show incredible. I said it wasn't difficult for me to portray Sipowicz in this aspect of his nature, that I could identify racist impulses in myself.

Later in the discussion I was asked about the character of Fancy, the black lieutenant played by James McDaniel. The questioner, who was black, felt that the character of Fancy was underutilized in our storytelling. I said that I agreed. When asked why Fancy wasn't used more, I pointed out that our storytelling priorities were different from the hierarchy of authority in the world of the 15th Squad. Simone and Sipowicz were at the show's center. On occasion, as we did with other secondary characters, we told stories which focused on Fancy; the rest of the time, he was an instrument of our storytelling needs in relation to the central characters.

Maybe disingenuously, I assumed that, since I was addressing a group of professional writers, I could speculate candidly about the realities of our business. I proposed that one reason so many television dramas portray black characters in positions of authority (the squad boss in every major police drama on commercial television is black) might be that these shows wanted to have the credentials of liberalism without having to portray in scope or depth minority characters with whom their writers were less comfortable or had less familiarity or whose fuller treatment they felt the audience might resist. I said that because I had less lived or observed experience on which to draw, I came to the portrayal of Fancy's character with less sense of imaginative authority than in writing other characters on the show.

The tone of some subsequent questions became combative. Was I saying I *enjoyed* writing a racist character? I said that one of writing's pleasures was giving yourself whole-souled in imagination to a different being, parts of whom you might have drawn from yourself.

I tried to analyze the process of writing a scene which began as an interview but turned into a confrontation between Sipowicz and a black man who had dated a white girl, a Bennington student who, because she was away at school, was the only surviving member of a wealthy white family all the rest of whom were killed in a home invasion.

The male black was a Ph.D. candidate at Hunter, and he deeply resented being questioned about any possible involvement in such a crime. Sipowicz explained to the man his belief that because the murders had occurred in lower Manhattan but fit exactly a pattern of home-invasion murders which had taken place in the Bronx, the perpetrators probably had only left their customary haunts because they'd known the layout of the residence which was their target. Accordingly, since several witnesses in the Bronx cases had mentioned seeing four black males fleeing the crime scenes, and since the black interviewee had dated the white girl who lived in the residence, Sipowicz wanted to know if the interviewee might have mentioned his having been in the house or what the house looked like to any of his friends.

"Oh, I get it," the interviewee responds. "I may not be a criminal, but y'get enough niggers together, some of them must be."

"Mr. Futrel," Sipowicz answers, "Rebecca said one of the reasons she broke up with you was you hung around with kind of a rough crowd. . . ."

The interviewee raises his voice over Sipowicz's. ". . . so I go to the *criminal* niggers and I say, 'Guess what—I'm bonin' this rich white girl, lemme tell you where she lives and where her mama hides her jewelry.' That the scenario you're envisioning, detective?"

Sipowicz considers the man. "Mr. Futrel. Have I been disrespectful to you?"

"*This* is disrespectful," Futrel answers. "Me being here."

Sipowicz loses his temper. "Hey, pal, I'm trying to find some assholes before they murder another innocent family. It happens these assholes are black. Now how do you want me to put the questions? 'I'm sorry for the injustices the white man has inflicted on your race, but can you provide any information?' 'I'm sorry your people have been downtrodden for three hundred years, but did you discuss the layout of the Sloan house with any of your friends?' "

Futrel won't back down. "Yeah," he says. "Do it that way."

"Okay," Sipowicz says. "I know that great African-American George Washington Carver discovered the peanut, but can you provide the names and addresses of these friends?"

Futrel glares at him. "You're a racist scumbag," he says.

"Ouch," Sipowicz replies.

I told the writers in the audience that I'd enjoyed Sipowicz's behavior in this scene. The corollary, which I should have mentioned but didn't, probably out of perversity or unconscious resentment at the accusatory tone of the question which had been put to me, was that I'd equally enjoyed writing the part of Futrel.

In another part of the discussion, one of the same questioners asked why there were so few black writers writing television drama. I proposed that in the area of drama, it was difficult for black American writers to write successfully for a mass audience. When they wrote out of the complexities of their own experience in full scope and detail, the result might be powerful and compelling as art but not commercially successful (*"I love it, but the audience doesn't tune in"*); yet, because their imaginations and interests had been so forged in the crucible of their racial experience, when, in order to avoid the imputation of parochialism, they tried to write what they thought the *white* audience wanted to hear, their writing might lose emotional thrust and drive.

I speculated that, to the extent such generalizations had any validity, the large number of Jews writing for television and other mass media might be accounted for by the difference between a Jewish writer's formative experiences and a black's. While both might grow up with that sense of doubleness in relation to mainstream American culture which affords storytelling distance, in recent generations the Jewish writer's experience had been much more benign and moderate than the traumatic sense of difference experienced by a black. Such writers therefore might not feel the dislocating sense of disloyalty to reality and self which a black writer might in writing neutrally about the mainstream culture.

I told of having organized a seminar several years before whose purpose was to expose minority writers to the process of writing for television. I'd hired someone to let students at black colleges around the country know that the seminar would be available in the coming summer, and to invite applications. From these we selected fifteen students and flew them to Los Angeles, providing them with housing and a stipend for the six weeks the seminar would last.

The seminar was also audited by a number of other writers, some minorities, some not, from Los Angeles.

I remarked that of those who'd attended the seminar, four had gone on to success as television writers, but none of these were black.

This was meant as analysis, not endorsement. I wanted the black writers in the audience to understand that if they chose to write for a mass medium, they should expect to be frustrated by the market's resistance to their work; to be prepared as well for self-doubt and self-division.

The press gave me an ass-kicking. *The Washington Post* was first to print a story about the talk, with the headline "Black and 'NYPD Blue'; Co-Creator Tells Seminar, 'I'm Racist.'" This earned me a happy phone call from Ted Harbert, head of ABC, who'd just been called by Jesse Jackson and wanted my version of what had happened before he called Reverend Jackson back. Meanwhile, *USA*

Today, The New York Times, and the *Chicago Tribune* printed their own accounts, which were followed by thoughtful treatments on *Entertainment Tonight* and CNN's *Hollywood Week.*

Steven, always a fan of my public pronouncements, issued a statement defending my worth as a person, reiterating the company's position on equal opportunity in hiring, and emphasizing that I'd told him my remarks had been taken out of context. This was Steven's distillation of what I'd actually said, which was that the quotes were accurate and everyone could go fuck themselves. The Fox public relations department then presented me with some copy they thought it would be useful to circulate over my name. The statement reiterated my commitment to equal opportunity in hiring and said that my remarks had been taken out of context, but that I regretted any hurt my words had caused. I told the public relations person I couldn't have said this better myself, which under the circumstances was obvious.

The following day, in his morning call, Jimmy Breslin told me that if I would now keep my mouth shut no matter what the press said to me, the story would be a one-week-wonder. Accordingly, I hung up the phone on *him.*

JIMMY WAS RIGHT ABOUT the story disappearing from the press, but the Humanitas session had several important aftereffects. James McDaniel was so disturbed by what he'd read and been told by friends of what I'd said that he procured and listened to a tape of the whole session. Before portraying Fancy, James had played parts I'd written for other shows; he believed that I wrote in good faith. But he asked me to consider whether by my own account, I hadn't acknowledged in the talk that he was a kind of second-class citizen, not only on the show, but in my imagination.

I also logged a lot of time on the telephone and answering letters from black writers. A number of these made the same point: because I was the executive producer of a respected and successful show, it was irresponsible of me to believe that I was simply offering food for thought; they were concerned that opinions I'd presented conjecturally might now be taken as a prescriptive justification for the hiring practices of other shows.

One letter was from a writer named David Mills, who congratulated me on guaranteeing the future employment of "so many mediocre white motherfuckers." David had, in fact, submitted a spec *NYPD Blue* script earlier in the year which one of our producers had described as marginally promising. In the crush of production, I'd used "marginally" as an excuse not to read it.

When a writer wants to be hired for the staff of a particular show, his agent invariably tells him to submit as his audition-script something he's written for a different series. The reasoning is that an *NYPD Blue* producer will identify more easily in an *NYPD Blue* script mischaracterizations or failures of understanding of the show's dramatic structure, and therefore will be more likely to reject the writer as a candidate for an assignment than the same producer would, say, on reading a spec-script for *Homicide,* or for *Law and Order.*

David didn't play this angle. He'd written an *NYPD Blue* script because that was the show he wanted to write for. His script *did* have some mischaracterizations and misunderstandings of our dramatic structure. But his scenes were vivid and credible. He wasn't afraid to try stories about people in emotional extremity, or to identify drama in small moments.

David was a keeper. He wrote the eighteenth script of our second season, for which Mark Tinker received an Emmy nomination as best director, and the opening script of the season about to begin.

Mr. Warren also used to say that life is never tidy. If I hadn't stuck my foot in my mouth, I'd never have read David's work.

AT THE HUMANITAS TALK, I remarked that when I'd finished the first draft of the script I've quoted from earlier in this chapter, I had a feeling of uneasiness. In that draft,

the main story ended with a second scene between Sipowicz and Lewis Futrel. Sipowicz had turned out to be right
that the perpetrators were black and had known the home's
layout, but wrong about how they'd gotten this information.
The white maid in the house, a secret drug-addict short
on money, had sold the floor plan to her dealer, who in
turn had sold it to the perpetrators who were also his
customers. Hearing that arrests had been made in the
case, Futrel comes back to the station house to confront
Sipowicz.

"I guess someone was doing some real detective work
while you stayed busy harassing me and my friends."

"I'm sorry you took it that way," Sipowicz replies.

"I want to hear you say you harassed me! I want to hear
you say me and my friends are not suspects—which Detective Andrew Sipowicz finds hard to believe, since we're
all just a bunch of low-life niggers!"

The volume and tone of Futrel's voice have brought
Fancy out of his office. He watches Sipowicz move a little
closer to the civilian.

"All right, Lewis. You made your little speech. You're
done now," Sipowicz says.

Futrel closes the distance between them. "I'm done
when I say I'm done."

"I'm telling you. You're done."

"I want to hear about George Washington Carver again, you ignorant cracker bigot."

At which point Fancy intercedes, telling Futrel his business in the squad room is finished. Futrel considers him with angry contempt.

"They letting you work in the Big House now, huh, boy? They let you come in the front door?"

"Leave now, Mr. Futrel," Fancy replies.

Futrel takes his parting shot at Sipowicz. "I'd love to take it one-on-one with you sometime, pal."

"Let me give you my card," Sipowicz replies.

I told the writers that something had felt wrong to me in the conclusion of the story. I had no problems with Sipowicz's behavior, which seemed to me true to his nature. But I recognized that, if the story ended here, not only would it take its final emotional stamp from Sipowicz's sensibility; it would also have portrayed Fancy as this sensibility's willing executioner. That wasn't true to *Fancy's* nature.

I added a scene in which Fancy, having casually invited Sipowicz out for an after-work sandwich, takes him to a rib joint. Sipowicz is the only white person in the place. On the cut, they're halfway through their meal.

"How's your food?" Fancy asks.

Sipowicz's puss is dour. "Good," he says.

"You try the slaw?" Fancy asks.

"You getting your jollies out of this, lieutenant?"

"What do you mean?"

"You think I'm a racist. You're rubbing my nose in it here a little bit. Well, let me tell you something, lieutenant. I'm entitled to my feelings and opinions as long as I do my job the right way. That investigation on that home-invasion went by the numbers. We had a description—four black men. . . ."

"Andy—"

"I questioned the girl did she have black acquaintances 'cause that was my suspect profile. I gave that Futrel guy zero noise till he got in my face."

"Andy. I think you handled the investigation properly."

"So what am I doing here?"

"Aren't you enjoying yourself?"

"Hey, lieutenant, let me know when you get done busting my balls."

"Is it the atmosphere, Andy?"

"Oh, that's possible. Something about me being the only white person here."

"Is it because you feel this isn't your place, and maybe some of these people think so too? Maybe a few of them just don't like you?"

"What's your point, lieutenant?"

"You're being served, aren't you, Andy? They cooked those ribs for you. Maybe they wanted to spit in the plate, but they didn't. They served your white ass just like they would anyone else who came in here. Even though some of them hate your guts. So why would you feel uncomfortable, Andy? You got your meal. What difference does it make what they're thinking? That they don't like you, that's just an opinion. Why should that bother you?"

Fancy considers Sipowicz, then asks "Now what if they had badges and guns?"

At which point the waiter brings the check, which Fancy grabs. "My treat," he tells Sipowicz.

I told the writers that what had made this new scene feel like the right ending had nothing to do with its more morally elevated perspective. I labored to make the point (and probably I'll labor making it now) that my sense of the earlier scene's inappropriateness as a conclusion had come not from my moral reservations about giving Sipowicz the last word, but from my sense of craft. As a writer I'd sensed that to end the story then would be to buy it on the cheap, that is, without having presented some act on Fancy's part that clarified his deeper feelings about what had transpired between Sipowicz and Futrel.

My point was that a commitment to craft had allowed me to overcome any defect of emotional commitment I might have to Fancy's character. I described how, as I was writing the scene, I began to feel Fancy come alive in my imagination, to speak with the same sort of specificity and out of the same depth of passion as Sipowicz and other characters to whom I came more easily. I said that coming to this heightened sense of Fancy's nature as I worked on the scene was what made me feel confident in assuring James McDaniel I *could* write and do justice to his character. I said that the opportunity to enlarge our spirits through pursuit of our craft was one of the blessings of our profession.

Natalie and Jennifer Clark (Bill's
daughters) with Dennis Franz and his
newly won Emmy

chapter 16

For me, Bill's being in Los Angeles full-time was a life-saver. He fielded many of the questions which came up from the set, and was invaluable in the preproduction tone meetings, where I'm supposed to go over our scripts page by page with the director, indicating how I think scenes should be played. My patience for these meetings is finite—my suggestions about scenes are on the order of "You know how to do this." Bill makes helpful and specific suggestions without being prescriptive (except in matters of police procedure, about which he's dogged to a point just short of intolerability).

Bill himself enjoyed his more consistent and unhurried participation in the making of the show. As he came to a better understanding of the different aspects of the process, he became more confident and took added responsibility, which taught him more still.

But Bill's adjustment to being off The Job and living away from New York was as difficult as we'd expected.

He loved his house, and enjoyed the process of slowly adding to the possessions his friend and fellow detective Mike Conroy had driven out in a U-Haul from New York. On Bill's time off, he and Rita would shop for crockery and antiques which would suit one or another of the rooms. And of course Bill had his menagerie of pets (he set up Steven's family room as his aviary).

He also liked spending time with Elizabeth, Ben, and Olivia. For their part, the children had some ambivalence about Bill's losing his status as a visitor because he'd always brought them such wonderful presents. He had dinner with us three or four times a week. Bill insisted on cooking one of these meals himself, although the fat and cholesterol in his concoctions kept me from partaking.

Bill found his other society with Dennis and, as time went on, Jimmy as well. And he made another friend in Billy Finklestein.

Billy is the writer-producer of *L.A. Law* and *Civil Wars*. He, Bill, and I had lunch almost every weekday in the studio commissary. One Monday, Billy told me about having gone with Bill the previous day to the pet store to pick out a bird for Billy's daughter Anna. The prospect of spending money brings out a preemptive belligerence in Bill. Billy Finklestein said that after he had explained to the salesman the kind of bird they were looking for (a Senegal parrot) and asked what such a bird would cost, the salesman, having a special affection for one of these parrots, pointed it out in the cage and began to describe the aspects of its behavior he especially enjoyed.

"So this is a bird with a story," Bill interrupted.

At this point, Billy Finklestein reported, the salesman fell silent.

"How much is the bird *without* the story?" Bill asked. "Just if we bought him plain."

The salesman named the price in a barely audible voice, and Billy Finklestein hurried to pay it. Bill insisted he hadn't been intimidating, but Billy Finklestein said he'd expected to open the Monday-morning paper and read that the salesman had hanged himself.

The truth was that, away from the set, Bill spent most of his time by himself.

ANYONE WHO ASKS BILL about women on The Job had better have time to spare. Bill doesn't think women should work as cops, insisting his objections are practical rather than sexist. He says women aren't strong enough to meet The Job's physical requirements, or to effect the intimidation which sometimes makes more direct forms of confrontation unnecessary.

Nevertheless, Bill once partnered for several years with a female detective named Karen Krizan. Karen went on to become a lieutenant, as well as president of the Policewoman's Endowment Association. (She once was featured on the cover of *New York* magazine.)

When I first began researching the show and wanted a woman's perspective on being a cop, Bill gave me Karen's name, and we spent an afternoon together. She'd been enormously helpful, and I'd made use of some of her stories. One of these was about a detective who couldn't understand Karen's objections to his coffee cup being adorned with ceramic, anatomically accurate breasts.

Several months after he'd moved to California, Bill told me that Karen had called him with the news her marriage had ended.

"Yeah, she might be coming out," Bill said. "There's that possibility."

Karen did come out, and she's been an increasingly frequent visitor. In fact, Bill has trouble finding time for us on his dinner calendar.

*   *   *

BILL'S BEAUTIFUL DAUGHTERS NATALIE and Jennifer also have come for several visits. The most recent of these was for the Golden Globe awards, where Dennis again won as best actor. *NYPD Blue* was nominated for best series, but *The X-Files* won. Afterward, Bill left Natalie and Jennifer for a moment to come to our table and ask me what the hell *The X-Files* was about.

Each of the nominated shows had been introduced with a thirty- or forty-second clip. The *X-Files* clip had showed a group of diminutive aliens probing an earthling with instruments. I was pissed off at our show's having lost and couldn't believe that with the clip just having been shown, Bill was asking me this question.

"Bosnia, Bill," I said. "Every week it's a different aspect on the War. One episode the Muslims and the Croats, then the Serbs and the Montenegrins . . ."

Bill considered me gravely a moment, then went back to his table.

It was a quiet car on the ride home. Rita and I were in the front seat, and Bill and his daughters were in the back. Finally, Bill tried to acquaint Natalie and Jennifer with the ways of Hollywood.

"See, this is the foreign press gives the Golden Globes. With best show, probably 'cause *X-Files* has that European setting, that's how they got the inside track."

After I got the car under control I asked Bill how in hell he could watch a clip filled with extraterrestrials sticking pins into an astronaut and think a show was about Bosnia. Bill said he'd been in the men's room when they'd showed the clip.

BILL HAS NEVER BEEN literal-minded about how we tell his stories. If we convey the emotional truth of a case he's worked on, he understands our rearranging or compressing its elements. He's also careful about identifying cases which weren't his. He names the cops who did work the case or who told him about a given incident. Our supply of such stories is tribute to Bill's friendships and the respect New York cops have for our show.

Bill's leaving The Job cut him off from active police work, but his moving to California and into Steven's house gave us a way to show our appreciation to his friends. Every few months we fly out colleagues of Bill's for three or four days of relaxing and sightseeing. (Bill now has a near-phobic reaction to the sight of Grauman's Chinese Theatre.) His friends stay at Bill's house, using it, in Bill's words, like a clubhouse. And I get to listen to them talk.

I could fill another book with stories I've heard from Chris Dowdell, Jimmy McGuire, Phil Panzarella, Johnny Wilde, Chris Deluca, Mike Conroy, and Jack Biesel. I'll tell just one of them, which was the basis for the script by David Mills which will open our third season.

Jack Biesel and his partner were on the street investigating a separate matter when they were approached by a Hispanic woman who frantically told them she was afraid her husband was being robbed. They lived on the second floor above a bar the husband operated, and he had been signaling her with a bell pulley he had rigged to let her know when there was trouble downstairs in the bar.

When Jack and his partner entered the bar they confronted an ambiguous scene. At the other end of the room the bartender and another man appeared to be in conversation. When Jack and his partner identified themselves as detectives this other man showed a shield of his own and said he was on The Job too. He took offense when they continued their approach with caution, asking if the fact he was black meant they couldn't trust a fellow cop who'd identified himself.

In the next instant another man appeared from behind the door and shot Jack Biesel in the chest. The shooter and the man who'd showed a shield fled. Jack and his partner gave chase, shooting at the two perpetrators as they ran across a vacant lot, but after fifty yards or so Jack went to his knees. He was in shock and bleeding badly. They called in their location and the direction in which the perpetrators had fled, and then his partner helped Jack back to their car and they started for the hospital.

They got about twenty blocks before Jack's partner slammed the car into a lamppost. The hood of the car flew up. It took Jack's partner a few minutes to get the hood down far enough to keep it from blocking his vision so they could start for the hospital again. When they arrived at the emergency entrance, Jack's partner pulled the car so close to the wall on the passenger's side that Jack couldn't get out. Then, backing the car up to put it at an angle where Jack could get out, he smashed into an arriving ambulance. Jack crawled out the window of the car and threw himself on a gurney. "All I want's a fighting chance," he said.

Cops from all over the city had converged on the crime scene. A resident on an upper floor of a nearby apartment building pointed to a Dumpster and said one of the perpetrators was hiding inside. Several uniform cops grabbed the fugitive up from the Dumpster and also found the gun he'd used. He was bleeding from a bullet wound in his right buttock and also from a head wound he'd incurred on coming into contact with a cinder block while being apprehended.

A detective took charge of driving the wounded perpetrator to the hospital. He brought him, hands cuffed behind his back, into the emergency room where the doctors were working on Jack Biesel. The detective, letting go of the perpetrator, who dropped to the floor, asked Biesel whether this was the cocksucker who had shot him. Biesel said it was.

An advance man for then-Mayor Koch came into the emergency room, saying the mayor had heard about the cop shooting and was on his way over. The advance man asked who the man was bleeding on the floor. When told this was the perpetrator, the advance man said to get him the hell out before the mayor came in. The detective put the perpetrator in a nearby storage closet.

Mayor Koch came in. He asked after Biesel, who said he was trying not to die. The physician in charge of Biesel's case returned to Biesel's bedside after having studied X rays of his chest. He said they'd been able to visualize the bullet; it was embedded in muscle near the heart and he didn't want to crack Biesel's chest to remove the bullet unless he had to. The doctor then asked why blood was seeping out from under the closet door and moved toward the door to investigate. The advance man herded Mayor Koch from the emergency room. The doctor opened the door and considered the man on the floor. He was told this was the perpetrator. "*This* man needs an operation," the doctor said.

Biesel would later learn that the perpetrator's rectum had been removed.

JACK TOLD OF HIS slow recovery from the shooting, and having come back to The Job, and learning how the other perpetrator had come to have a shield: he was a corrections officer who used parolees he'd met when they were jailed at Rikers to help him pull stickups. Although the gun had been used by the other perpetrator, it belonged to the corrections guard and was traced back to him.

Biesel said that after eighteen months he finally learned why the corrections guard still hadn't gone to jail. He'd been working undercover for the District Attorney's Office making cases against *other* corrupt guards. The DA's staff didn't want to lose him as their operative or lose the time and money they'd invested in the operation.

One day at court, Biesel saw the detective who had brought the wounded perpetrator into the emergency room. The detective asked him how the prosecution was going against the two men who had shot him. Biesel said the one guy had gone to jail and why the other guy hadn't.

"That's no fucking good," the detective said. "A cop gets shot and these pricks deal?"

The detective went to a newspaper friend and leaked the story. When it ran, the DA pulled the plug. The corrections officer went to jail.

"Billy took all that trouble, and he didn't even know me that good," Jack Biesel said. "He just didn't think it was right."

*   *   *

"BILLY," OF COURSE, WAS Bill. That night, after we'd taken Jack and his friends to the airport for their flight back to New York, I asked Bill why he hadn't prompted Biesel to tell the story earlier in his visit.

Bill said he hadn't thought about it.

I looked at him. "Are you telling me you'd have let him leave without telling me that story? How could you ask him out here and not make him tell me that?"

"I'll tell you the truth," Bill said. "I really wanted to have Jack out here 'cause I forgot to invite him to the Palm Shore that night, when we had the racket for our premiere."

I KEEP TO A strict diet now, and exercise every day. (I try to get Bill to exercise with me, but he says the treadmill gives him shin splints.) I've lost fifty pounds, but I'm not sure this doesn't fall under the category of improving barn security after the farm creatures have headed for the meadow.

Whatever happens, I've got no complaints. I've gotten the chance to do honorable work, and to love and be loved by my family, and my friend Bill.

acknowledgments

From David Milch—

My thanks to Bernadette McNamara and Ray Cochran for their assistance in the writing of this book, and to Claire Wachtel and Lisa Bankoff for helping to conceive its premise. Also to Drs. Arvid Underman, Drew Pinsky, John Easthope, Peter Pelikan, Timothy Hays, Irwin Friedman, Jeffrey Schwartz, Phillip Sullivan, and Patrick Whitlow for their kind and effective care.

Loving gratitude to my brother, Bob, and his family and our mother, Mollie, and to my teachers, especially Steven Bochco.

From Bill Clark—

First of all, I'd like to thank my mom and dad, my sister Barbara, and my lovely daughters, Natalie and Jennifer, for always being there for me.

I'd like to thank the members of the New York City Police Department for allowing me to serve with them for twenty-five wonderful years, which gave me the experiences that have opened up this door for me. To the wonderful partners I had during those years, whom I will not name for fear of neglecting to mention one of them.

I also wish to thank my friends John Giglio, Henny Ryan, Tony Grimaldi, Frank Dougherty, Sean Driscoll, Ed Downe, Larry Ponzi, and Morris and Rachel Goldman for giving me personality traits to emulate. Pat Corr, Raymond Miu, and Charlie Healy for having the patience to deal with the uncertainties of my schedule and still giving me a day's work so as to make my family's life a little easier.

To former Commissioner Ray Kelly for having the faith in me to bring me back to the Police Department and rejuvenating my life.

To Claire Wachtel for having the faith she did in this project.

To Nicole Ross for sharing with me difficult times in both our lives.

To Dick Schaap for never saying no to a friend. To my friend Jimmy Breslin for making it unnecessary for me to have an alarm clock for twenty years.

To Steven Bochco for allowing me into his devoted and loyal production company and for giving me the self-confidence to make such a dramatic career change.

To Rita, Elizabeth, Benjamin, and Olivia for allowing me into their home and their lives.

To Karen for her love, faith, and support.

To Michael Daly for being a friend and introducing me to David Milch, who has taken the place of my brother John in all of my future plans.